OTHER BOOKS BY KENNON L. CALLAHAN

A New Beginning for Pastors and Congregations

Building for Effective Mission

Dynamic Worship

Effective Church Finances

Effective Church Leadership

Giving and Stewardship in an Effective Church

Preaching Grace

Small, Strong Congregations

Twelve Keys for Living

Twelve Keys to an Effective Church

Twelve Keys to an Effective Church: The Leaders' Guide

Twelve Keys to an Effective Church: The Planning Workbook

Twelve Keys to an Effective Church: The Study Guide

Visiting in an Age of Mission

The Future
That Has Come

The Future That Has Come

New Possibilities for Reaching and Growing the Grass Roots

∞

Kennon L. Callahan

JOSSEY-BASS
A Wiley Company
San Francisco

Published by

JOSSEY-BASS
A Wiley Company
989 Market Street
San Francisco, CA 94103-1741

www.josseybass.com

Jossey-Bass books and products are available through most bookstores.
To contact Jossey-Bass directly, call (888) 378-2537, fax to (800) 605-2665,
or visit our website at www.josseybass.com. Substantial discounts on bulk
quantities of Jossey-Bass books are available to corporations, professional
associations, and other organizations. For details and discount information,
contact the special sales department at Jossey-Bass.

We at Jossey-Bass strive to use the most environmentally sensitive
paper stocks available to us. Our publications are printed on acid-free
recycled stock whenever possible, and our paper always meets or
exceeds minimum GPO and EPA requirements.

Unless otherwise stated, biblical quotations are from *The Holy Bible,
Revised Standard Version* (copyright © 1965 Thomas Nelson & Sons).

Library of Congress Cataloging-in-Publication Data
Callahan, Kennon L.
  The future that has come: new possibilities for reaching and
growing the grass roots / Kennon L. Callahan.
    p. cm.
    Includes index.
    ISBN 0-7879-4981-7 (alk. paper)
    1. Church. I. Title.
    BV600.2 .C327 2002
    253—dc21   2001004960

FIRST EDITION
HB Printing   10 9 8 7 6 5 4 3

Contents

Acknowledgments

This book is for congregations, pastors, and leaders looking forward to living in the future that has come. It is for people who seek to build strong, healthy lives and strong, healthy congregations in the grace of God. It is for people who want to reach and grow the grassroots.

As the dedication shows, I want to thank my high school class and Sarah Polster.

First, Sarah. I want to thank her for her contributions to my life. Sarah was the editor of four of my best books, and she was to have been the senior editor of this book, too. We had looked forward to sharing in the project together. Early into the project, I called the publisher to visit with Sarah. Her editorial assistant shared with me the news of Sarah's very serious illness. Julie and I felt a deep sadness for a good friend whose promise of life was in jeopardy. Sarah struggled with her illness for many months. At one point, she seemed to be getting better. Sadly, a turn for the worse came. We received word of Sarah's death as this book was being completed.

Over the years, I have had the privilege of working with some of the finest, most competent people on the planet. Sarah was remarkable with her wisdom, insight, clarity, and creativity. Her gifts with words, sentences, and meanings are the best I have ever known. The books she edited were the pride of her life. They benefit thousands of people and congregations across the planet.

She had a wonderful daughter in Anna. She was married to Michael. She was a gifted mother and wife. Her family was the joy of her life. Her gifts of thoughtfulness and kindness touched the lives of many people. Her gentle leadership and her perceptive intelligence lifted up the people with whom she lived and worked. Her spirit of compassion and sense of hope blessed all of us.

I write these words of appreciation, first to honor Sarah for who she was, for her remarkable gifts, and for the amazing contributions she made in people's lives. I also write these words in the hope that someday her daughter will read them and know, even more fully than she can at her current young age, how wonderful, gifted, wise, and creative her mother really was.

I am thankful that Sarah and I could work together on the four recent books. I am most grateful for who she was and for her remarkable contributions. Julie and I wish Anna and Mike the blessings of God's grace and hope. Our prayers join those of countless friends and family.

Second, I want to thank the members of my high school class, the Cuyahoga Falls High School Class of 1954, for their contributions to my life. In recent years, I have come to realize how much the individuals in my high school class, and indeed the class as a whole, have contributed to my life.

We were fortunate to grow up in Cuyahoga Falls, Ohio. Mostly, it was a peaceful, happy community, not too large, not too small. Tree-lined streets and good parks. Waterworks was the community swimming pool, fed by cold artesian well water, built in WPA days, twenty-five meters wide and one hundred meters long. I served as lifeguard there for several summers.

Front Street gathered most of the shops in town. There was a movie theater, and next to it the A&P, the first supermarket, started and managed by my Dad. We had strong, healthy congregations, three of which share a large park of land near Front Street. We went to a good high school, benefited from solid teachers, and largely grew and matured together with a healthy, creative spirit.

As a high school class, we had our share of troubles and despair, tragedies and disappointments. We grieved when classmates died so young. We sensed how precious and precarious life is. In good times, we celebrated, richly, fully, our accomplishments and achievements. We loved one another, disagreed and fought with one another, made up, talked about one another, and closed ranks with one another. We were bright and smart. We were articulate, purposeful, and constructive. On occasion, we wondered at our good luck to live and grow up in the time in which we did. We were a fun class. We enjoyed life. Our high school years were good years.

In the time come and gone, in my work and travels, I have had the privilege of knowing many high school classes. As high school classes go, we were fortunate to be in our class. We are among the best I know. I am grateful for how my high school class encouraged me to advance the gifts with which God has blessed me. As I look back, I see even more clearly the encouraging spirit, the compassion, the good fun, the remarkable events of growing and discovering that we shared.

Some people bring out the best in those around them. My high school class is like that. I am grateful they helped to bring out the best in me. I am thankful for the contributions they are making to help the world be a better place in which to live. In their families, communities, work, and lives, they are contributing to the quality of life we all share on this planet. I am thankful God surrounded me with the classmates who became the Class of 1954. I have been most fortunate.

I want to thank Julie McCoy Callahan. God's greatest gift in my life is Julie. We are good friends. We enjoy being with one another. We love one another. She brings wisdom and compassion, understanding and love to my life. She is the most remarkable, the most encouraging person I know. Her gentle spirit, her wonderful sense of joy, and her marvelous creativity are extraordinary gifts in my life, and in the lives of all she touches.

She is a legend across the planet.

Countless people work with her, by telephone, letter, and in person, to advance the mission we share. The seminars, books, and consultations are all made possible through her gifted leadership. The movement we began, the Mission Growth Movement, is the better for her gifts, leadership, and compassion.

I want to thank D'Wayne Roberts. She has contributed much to the development of this book, as well as most of the others. She has done the typing and the first edit of the original manuscript. Her precision and accuracy are remarkable. Her suggestions for the manuscript were most helpful. Her spirit of generosity and goodwill found their way into the final book. I am grateful that D'Wayne, Julie, and I share this life together as good friends.

I want to thank Tom Finnegan. He is a gifted person. Tom has served as copyeditor for *The Future That Has Come*. We have come to know one another through our work together on this book. He stands with Sarah as among the most competent people with whom I have the privilege of sharing and working. He has contributed his wonderful gifts of clarity, thoughtfulness, and wisdom to the development of the book. It is a strong, helpful book because of his contributions.

I want to thank Chandrika Madhavan. As Sarah's administrative assistant, Chandrika has done triple duty during Sarah's illness. She has made significant contributions to bringing the book to fulfillment. Julie and I appreciate her kindness, effectiveness, and good spirit. Across the years, I have known many outstanding administrators. She is among the best. Jossey-Bass is fortunate to have her.

I want to thank Joanne Clapp Fullagar. Each time we talk by telephone we have a wonderful time. She and her team are responsible for bringing this book to publication. Her attention to the overall production, workflow, and needed details to produce an excellent book is remarkable. Her spirit of goodwill, generosity, and helpfulness is a gift to all. Her competencies and her friendship are gifts of God.

I want to thank Andrea Flint. She has served as production editor for the book. She is a wonderfully competent person. Her training and background are excellent. She has a generous spirit. Her attention to detail is remarkable. This is the first book on which we have worked together. I am grateful for her competencies, thoughtfulness, and outstanding contributions. It is fortunate that Jossey-Bass has the benefit of her gifts and abilities.

I want to thank the entire group of people that make Jossey-Bass the excellent publisher it is. A publishing company is no stronger than the team of people who work for it. There are many publishers on the planet. Jossey-Bass continues to be among the very best. I am grateful for the wonderful spirit and outstanding competencies that are present at Jossey-Bass.

I want to thank the congregations, leaders, and pastors who have contributed so much to my understanding of this distinctive time God has given us. The many participants in the seminars, workshops, and lectureships have given much to me in their solid questions, their excellent ideas, and their good suggestions.

I am amazed at the countless friendships, across the whole of the planet, with which we are blessed. We share a remarkable journey together. We learn from one another. We learn with one another. I am grateful that, together, we are blessed to live in this new age.

I encourage you to have fun with the book. You will find it enjoyable, encouraging, helpful. The wisdom and possibilities will benefit you. God bless you, your family, your mission, and your congregation in this remarkable new time.

∞

A further word.

The Calamities in New York, Washington, D.C., and Pennsylvania on September 11, 2001, remind us that there is much trouble and evil in this world. These terrible, sad events stir our anguish and anger, our despair and determination.

This is a time for movements. Some movements are strong, healthy, and constructive. They contribute to the advance of humanity. People discover whole, healthy lives in the grace of God. Some movements are destructive, demonic, and evil. They bring ruin and wreckage, terror and tears, sorrow and mourning.

God gives us hope. God gives us the assurance that Easter is stronger than Good Friday, the open tomb is stronger than the bloodied cross, resurrection is stronger than crucifixion. Amidst the travails and troublements that come, God leads us to new life and hope. We have this confidence. We will discover the strengths with which God is blessing us. We will sense the hope of God in dark, tragic times. We will discover the forgiveness of God in sinful times. We will discover the grace of God. We will discover the future God is giving us as a gift. We will serve well the mission to which God invites us. Current events make even more important an understanding of the seven major paradigm shifts that have happened in recent times. May God bless your mission.

KENNON L. CALLAHAN
November 2001

The Future
That Has Come

1

Movement

*Then I saw a new heaven and a new earth . . . for the former
    things have passed away.
And he who sat upon the throne said, "Behold, I make all
    things new."*

—Revelation 21:1, 4, 5

The future has come. God has given us a new time. We have
arrived at a new shore. We have come to a new world. The
morning sun has shone on a new day. There is a time for new
beginnings. There is a time for old ways. This is a time for
new beginnings. Welcome to a new age. God has blessed us.
God has given us seven major paradigm shifts, with new possibilities for reaching and growing the grass roots.

A New Time

This book confirms what has happened. This is not a book of
emerging trends to come in some distant time, nor is it a book
of strident prophecy of things terrible yet to be. This book confirms with you the new, encouraging future that has happened in our lifetime—indeed, in the recent years of our
lives. This book confirms the new possibilities God has given
congregations for the new day in which we now live.

We are in this new time not because of a century change or a millennial change, however celebrative they may be. To be sure, they do contribute to the sense, the anticipation, the expectancy of a new time, but a century or millennium change is not, in itself, sufficient to confirm what has happened in our time. We are in this new time because, in recent years, these seven paradigm shifts have happened. In this new time, God has given us these possibilities: movement, compassion, stars, sprinters, mission, creativity, and whole.

We look to the future. We discover it is already here. It has already happened. Yes, we look to the future so we know what to do in the present. The purpose of looking ahead is not to know what to do tomorrow, or even what one might do next year, but to know what to do today. We look forward to know what to do in the present.

Now, as we look ahead, we discover, with joy and wonder, surprise and amazement that the future—remarkably, extraordinarily—has come to pass in our time. We now live in one of the richest new ages humankind has ever known. We have not experienced one or two paradigm shifts; God has given us seven. They have reshaped the present and the future, for centuries to come.

This is not a post-Christendom time, as fortunate as that would be. Some people bemoan the thought of a post-Christendom time. With distress, they lament and grieve, weep and wail that the church is no longer central to the culture. They enjoyed the prestige, the perks, the pedestal of the church in that churched culture time. However, the church is never quite at home with the prestige and power of a Christendom time. In such times, the church becomes bloated and bureaucratic, lazy and indifferent. The church was born in a manger, not a mansion. The church is always at its blazing best in a time of mission.

This is not a new dark ages time. Some people have suggested such a thought. However, this makes an assumption about how dark the earlier dark ages were. Further, even if those dark ages were really that dark, we are not in a time of dark ages. We are in a new beginnings time. Yes, many old ways have passed away. Many familiar customs are no more. What may seem dark is simply God's way of inviting us to move on to the new future that has come, the new age that God has given to us.

We live in a megadigm time. I invented this term to describe the remarkable time in which we live. A megadigm is a time when there is a convergence of multiple paradigm shifts, interacting simultaneously with one another and therefore creating a new age, a markedly new time in the course of human history and human development. It is as though seven dynamic atomic particles of differing shape, size, and energy are interacting with one another. The result is a new creation, a new element, a new substance, a new age.

In a way, every age is a new time. In each age of human history, people have thought of their time as a new time. They were correct. Each generation, each age, fashions its own way. Each creates a new present that matches its own strengths. Moreover, some ages are "more" new. The fall of Rome in 410 A.D. was such a time. Some times are newer than other times. The rise of the Protestant Movement in 1517 A.D. was such a time. Some ages are "new new." The birth of Christ was such a time.

Some people talk, appropriately, of a paradigm shift at a given point in human history. As we look back on the history of humanity, we can see times when a paradigm shift has happened. We do not live in a time of one paradigm shift. We live in one of the rare, remarkable times of humankind when a number of paradigm shifts are happening at the same time.

We are living in a time when the future has come in a distinctive, extraordinary new form, a new form that humankind has never seen before.

These major paradigm shifts have happened in our time:

1. The shift from institution to movement

2. The shift from commitment to compassion

3. The shift from this planet to the stars

4. The shift from a solid marathon runner culture to an excellent sprinter culture

5. The shift from top-down maintenance to grassroots mission

6. The shift from controlling and directing to creativity and objectives

7. The shift from focus on the parts to focus on the whole

These major paradigm shifts, given of God, provide us with new possibilities for reaching and growing the grass roots. Strong, healthy congregations live these qualities: movement, compassion, stars, sprinters, mission, creativity, and whole. They reach and grow the grass roots.

Institution to Movement

There is a time for movements. There is a time for institutions. This is the time for movements. In this new time, healthy congregations live as movements. They have the confidence and assurance that one way of reaching and growing the grass roots is thinking, planning, behaving, and living as a movement.

The invitation came—for Friday and Saturday, October 1 and 2. Julie and I discussed whether we could go. We discovered we could arrange our schedules to do so. We knew it would be fun. People would be coming from across the country. We would see friends we had not seen in a long time. It would be a happy gathering.

We would gather in our hometown, Cuyahoga Falls, Ohio. This gracious, small town is at its best in October. During this month, it is one of the most beautiful places on our planet. The autumn tree colors are extraordinary. The leaves have turned to their rust and golden brilliance. The weather is splendid. Gentle breezes have cooled the summer heat and humidity. There is expectancy in the air as people look to the celebrations of Halloween, Thanksgiving, and Christmas.

Crowds assemble in the high school football stadium on Friday nights to watch the Tigers play their best football. The cheerleaders exalt the crowd. The marching band does its show at halftime. There is an excitement and peace, enthusiasm and quiet beauty, expectancy and contentment about the month of October in Cuyahoga Falls. We would gather at the beginning of that month.

Julie and I both grew up in this small town nestled at the bend of the Cuyahoga River Gorge. As children, we spent many happy times playing in the gorge. We did not know one another at the time, but each of us has fond memories of those explorations. Julie and her friend, Sue Swain, along with others, investigated the trails and paths of the gorge. Richard Barr and I did the same. We were especially interested in the caves, the cliffs, and the river. It is a wonder our paths—Julie's and mine—did not cross in those early years.

In our growing-up time, Cuyahoga Falls was a small town with one high school and several elementary schools. Broad Street, divided by its plush, green median of grass and trees, and Portage Trail were the two major east-west avenues. Front Street, running north and south, was the downtown of our time. State Road had just begun to develop as a second major north-south road, with shopping centers and stores emerging. In our years there, Front Street, with its A&P store, founded by my dad, and its movie theater next door, along with the other shops, were the primary gathering places of the town.

On Saturdays, during the years of World War II, our family would make a grand expedition, first to the A&P; then later we would go to the movie theater. My mother, younger brother, and I lived on the first floor of a triplex on Myrtle Avenue, located on the east side of the river. My dad was away fighting in the war in the Pacific.

My grandmother and my young cousins Lynn, Nancy, and Valerie lived on the second floor. Their dad, my uncle, was fighting in the war in Europe. Their mother had died. We were doing the best we could to keep the family together during the war. My grandmother looked after the girls, and we all helped one another. We rented out the third floor for some income.

On Saturdays, all of us would walk from the east side of the river, along Portage Trail, down the hill, across the river bridge, and come up to Front Street. From there, we would head to the A&P Supermarket to buy our food for the coming week. After we did our shopping, we would load the groceries into our large red wagon, head back down Portage Trail, across the river, up the other hill, to our home on Myrtle Avenue. We would put away all the groceries.

Then, as our treat for the week, we would walk back down the hill, across the river, and up the hill to the movie theater. There, with bags of warm, buttered popcorn, we would see two full-length features, the serial, the cartoons, and the newsreel of the world.

In his play *Our Town*, Thornton Wilder describes Grover's

Corners. Our own town, Cuyahoga Falls, was in those times much like Grover's Corners. When the train came through at night, most people were in bed. It was a peaceful, mostly quiet community. Living in Cuyahoga Falls, we grew up in pleasant surroundings, in a wonderful town, with good friends and family.

Julie and I arrived on Thursday, October 1, with a sense of anticipation and expectancy. We were getting together to celebrate the forty-fifth anniversary of my graduation at the class of 1954 high school reunion. On Friday and Saturday, we had fun visiting informally with old friends and discovering some new friends in spouses we had not met in the years come and gone. The town was having a festival on Front Street. We enjoyed the booths and shows.

The highlight of the reunion was the banquet on Saturday night. We had a wonderful time laughing, carrying on, visiting with one another. The meal prepared by the Sheraton Hotel was excellent. Julie and I were fortunate to sit at a table filled with many of our long-lost friends.

Dick Weber served as chair. Marilyn Albers, Billie Kennedy, Leona Krisher, Betty Moss, and Patsy Orozco served as the committee. They did a remarkable job of planning the reunion. Their leadership, wisdom, generosity, and thoughtfulness created one of the most remarkable, memorable events of our lives.

Dick was master of ceremonies for the evening. Following the dinner, there were the customary announcements, the words of thank-you, the taking of the class picture, the remarks by our class officers, and the remembrances of those who had died. Somewhere in that mix, Dick called on me to share the Class Tribute, which I had written for the reunion. As the days, weeks, and years—forty-five strong—passed before all our eyes, these are the words I shared.

A Tribute to the Class of 1954

We are the Class of 1954.
Time has passed.
Years have come and gone.
It seemed only yesterday. It is today.
We have lived and live on.

We are blessed.
We grew up in a good place in a good time.
We went to good schools.
We had mostly good teachers.

The depression marked our early years.
War touched our families.
Some went off to battle. Some came home. Some did not.

We resolved to rebuild the world and we did.
The world is better for our work.
We have done well.
We are ready to greet the new century, the new millennium.

We have seen success and loss.
We know health and illness.
Despair and grief come to us.
Wonder and joy are with us.

We have seen good times and rugged times.
Tears and sorrow have found us.
Trouble and difficulty are not strangers.
Hope is our good friend.

We have loved and been loved.
We have felt lost and lonely.
We have made some excellent mistakes.
We have learned.

Marriages have flourished. Children have been born.
Divorces have happened. Grandchildren quicken our lives.
We have worked hard. We are discovering retirement.
Death visits us. New life comes.

We remember, now, those whose lives ended so soon.
They will not grow old,
as we who are left grow old together.
We remember them with love and affection.

We have laughed. We have cried.
We have shared good fun and good times.
We have known tough, tragic times.
Defeat has found us. We discover hope.

We gather to celebrate 45 years.
We look older. We look the same.
We see old friends. We discover new.
We are amazed at who we are and who we have become.

We are the class of love and hope.
We are the class of generosity and compassion.
We have lived well. We are living well.
We will live well in the years to come.

We are among the best of the best.
Well done, Class of 1954!

That night, as I was sharing the tribute, it came to me: *we are the generation whose life span has bridged the major cultural shift from a time of institutions to a time of movements.* Many generations have lived during a time of institutions. Some generations have lived during a time of movements. We are among the few generations across the course of human history that have lived from a time of institutions through the transition to a time of movements.

Many institutions do good work. The Marshall Plan that rebuilt Europe after World War II was an institutional, organizational, bureaucratic way of rebuilding Europe. The point is this: it worked. Europe was rebuilt. One can point to the enormous contributions that many institutional, organizational, bureaucratic ventures made to advance humankind during those years following the war. They were remarkable achievements.

It came to me that night. The discovery has stayed with me ever since. The night was memorable for the gathering of friends. It was remarkable for the discovery I made. Our class has been privileged to live during one of the major transition shifts in the course of humankind. We have lived from a time of institutions to a time of movements.

Qualities of a Movement and Qualities of an Institution

In our time, people are drawn to a movement, not an institution. In an earlier time, people were drawn to institutions. Institutions had compelling value, and people invested considerable time, energy, effort, strengths, gifts, and competencies in advancing those institutions. Now, people are drawn to movements rather than institutions. For most people in our time, the compelling interest is to participate in a movement, not an institution.

If the *Star Wars* movies had been made in an earlier time, the ending would have been different. Take the time of the British Empire at its height. If the movie had been made back then, at the end of the movie the empire would have won. Most of the audience would have cheered. It was a time of institutions, a time of empires. The empire had commanding importance. Across the course of human history, one discovers times in which institutions have had compelling value. People invested their lives in strengthening and supporting the institutions of their time.

For centuries upon centuries, the institution of the pharaohs of Egypt had compelling value. The peoples of that time viewed the empire with a lasting reverence. The institutional character of that long-lost empire lasted for thousands of years. The exodus, the movement of the people of Israel, went forth from that institution.

Later, the institution of the Roman Empire had compelling value. The empire glued the fabric of human civilization across the Mediterranean for longer than people could remember. The phrase "Rome is eternal" caused merchants to sail, armies to march, roads to be built, and an established order for civilization to be put in place.

Subsequently, following the fall of Rome in 410 A.D., the institution of the Roman church in the West sought to bring a compelling sense of order to civilization. It was valiant in its efforts to nurture the recapitulation of the Roman Empire with the Holy Roman Empire of that later time. The institution of St. Peter held forth with its sale of indulgences to build a cathedral in Rome. This, among other causes, precipitated the movement of Martin Luther. He brought us to a new time beyond the institution of Rome.

Later, the institution of the British Empire held sway across the planet. It was said, "The sun never sets on the British Empire." The formidability of the institution of the British Empire was remarkable. In 1776, the American Revolution was an effort by a group of people who were drawn to a movement rather than to the almost overpowering institution of that time. The movement of John Wesley led beyond the institutions of his time. Across the course of human history, there have been times of institutions, and there have been times of movements.

In our day, people are drawn to a movement, not an institution. People join a congregation, not a denomination. People join a family, not an organization. People join a movement, not an institution. Movements focus on people. Institutions focus on policies. Congregations develop people. Institutions develop programs.

In this time, people look for three things in a congregation: help, hope, and home. They want to share and give, as well as receive and benefit. They want to help, not simply to be helped. They want to be sources of hope, not simply receivers of hope. They count on helping to create a sense of home, of roots, place, and belonging, as well as being included in the family of a congregation.

Ernst Troeltsch lived from 1865 to 1923. For most of his adult years, he taught in Augsburg in the fields of theology and philosophy. Troeltsch developed what is sometimes referred to as the sect-church typology. His thesis was that every sect becomes a church. Splintering off from that church is a new sect that eventually becomes a church. Splintering off from that church is a new sect that ultimately becomes a church.

Over the course of the Christian movement, there is evidence of this dynamic. One can see the Wesleyan sect splintering off from the Church of England. One can see that sect becoming the Methodist church. Then one can see the Nazarene sect splintering off from the Methodist church. There are countless examples.

I am grateful to Troeltsch for the help he has given me. His research encouraged me to explore my own research and reflections and led me to advance my own perspective. Yes, it

From Sect to Church

Sect → Church → Sect → Church → Sect → Church

is helpful to consider the sect-church typology, but we are not simply discussing the dynamics of a sect and a church. In a larger sense, it is more helpful to know we are looking at a movement-institution typology. We are seeing the unfolding of the dynamics of a movement and the behavior of an institution.

Movements think, plan, behave, act, and live in certain ways. The same is true of institutions. Moreover, it is not inevitable that every movement turn into an institution. An example that comes to mind is the Alcoholics Anonymous movement. It has a built-in tradition that makes the likelihood of it taking on the character of an institution remote. The "each one–teach one" movement multiplies itself across the planet, hardly noticed and powerfully present.

In our time, a movement is more compelling than an institution. Institutions are compelling, but now a movement is more compelling. Many of the institutions of our time will continue and will contribute to the health and well-being of humankind. I am simply confirming that now people are drawn to a movement, not an institution.

The simplest way to compare the qualities of a movement and the qualities of an institution is to look at a list. I describe these as clues, as hints, as qualities. As you look through these clues, think of you and of your congregation. Which of these describe the way you think, plan, feel, dream, act, behave, and live? You can use the list by putting a check next to the qualities, in one column or the other, that in fact describe how you and your congregation think and live.

For example, your congregation may emphasize the qualities of love, encouraging, forgiving, and sharing. Put checks by these qualities. A congregation may stress obligation, correcting, duty, and loyalty, and it would put checks by those qualities. As best you can, put your checks by qualities that describe how you actually think, plan, feel, act, and live.

Movement	**Institution**
Relational	Functional
Informal	Formal
Relaxed	Systematic
Being	Doing
Spontaneous	Organized
Flexible	Bylaws
Loosely developed	Planned
Casual gatherings	Regular meetings
Love	Obligation
Encouraging	Correcting
Forgiving	Duty
Sharing	Loyalty
Hope	Memory
New life	Old ways
Present	Past
Forward	Back
Grace	Law
Possibilities	Policies
Discoveries	Procedures
Yea-saying	Naysaying
At edge of resources	Conserving, holding
External, in world	Internal, in church
Mission	Maintenance
Resourcing	Retrenching
Service, serving	Survival, self-serving
Short-term mission teams	Long-term committees
Helping people discover power	Accumulating power
God's missionaries together	Caste system of laity and clergy

In this time, strong, healthy congregations think, plan, behave, and live as a movement. They do so with a spirit of consistency and creativity, a sense of reliability and continuity. They do not think and live the characteristics of an institution. The values on which they focus, the qualities they share, and the patterns by which they live are those of a movement.

An effective congregation delivers the qualities of a movement with consistency and creativity, reliability and continuity. A weak, declining congregation or a dying congregation delivers the qualities of an institution with consistency and creativity, reliability and continuity. It is difficult for a congregation to do both. It cannot go back and forth between the qualities of a movement and the qualities of an institution— now thinking and valuing one way, then thinking and valuing another.

To exist at all, a grouping has to deliver, however fragile and feeble, some sense of consistency and creativity, reliability and continuity. A bifurcation does not work. A congregation cannot one moment behave like a movement, and in the next moment behave like an institution. A congregation chooses one set of qualities or the other. It may do so consciously, or unconsciously. The choice may be intentional, or habitual.

Consider which qualities best describe how you and your congregation think, plan, behave, feel, dream, act, and live together.

For example, strong congregations think, plan, behave, and live in such a way that they are always living at the edge of their resources. These congregations have compelling value with the grass roots precisely because of their spirit of serving. Healthy congregations, of whatever size—small, strong, medium, large, regional, or mega—are always giving away more in volunteers, talents, strengths, gifts, competencies, and money than they have. Their focus is on advancing and serving God's mission. They trust God to provide resources to match the mission they generously share in the community and across the planet.

By contrast, when I am with a weak and declining congregation, or with a dying congregation, I discover that its focus is on the qualities of an institution. It is not accidental that the congregation is weak and declining or dying. The qualities of an institution may have had compelling value in an earlier time. They do not have compelling value in this time. People are not drawn to an institutional congregation that has a conserving, holding, protecting, and preserving stance toward whatever resources, strengths, gifts, and competencies it may have.

In an institutional, organizational, bureaucratic church, some leader will stand and tell the congregation, "We want you to know we are doing the best we can to conserve and hold, protect and preserve our church's meager financial resources." What this statement tells everyone in the congregation to do is conserve and hold, protect and preserve their own meager financial resources. Further, it teaches all the people in the community that this is an institution committed to conserving and holding, protecting and preserving its meager resources.

Another example helps. In an institutional, organizational, bureaucratic church, much is made of the caste system between clergy and laypeople. Much is made of the distinctive character of ordination. There is a subtle, hierarchical tendency in an institutional church. There is a sense in which the church communicates that "clergy" have a slightly higher stance in relationship to laity. I have lost track of the number of times someone has said to me, "Well, after all, I'm only just a layperson."

By contrast, in a healthy, effective congregation that thinks and plans, behaves and lives as a movement, everyone is viewed as God's missionary. There is no caste system. There is no higher or lower. There is a clear understanding of the diversity of gifts. No gifts are considered better or higher than other gifts. The spirit is that "we are all in this together, and we all contribute based on the gifts with which God blesses us."

In the television series *M*A*S*H*, most of the team knew they were at the front lines. Helicopters were bringing in the wounded. Everyone helped each other. Frank was the only one who was engrossed in a caste-system distinction between officers and soldiers. He was preoccupied with the prestige, the pedestal, and the power of being an officer. Everyone else on the team pitched in. There was no time to be preoccupied with the prestige, the pedestal, and the power.

The wounded needed care; the dying needed comfort. Everyone needed to function together as a team to give that comfort and care. Likewise, a healthy congregation plans, behaves, and lives as a movement. There is the spirit that we are in this together. We are God's missionaries, advancing God's mission in our community and across the planet.

The Manger and the Movement

The movement begins in a manger, not a mansion. The movement begins in a stable, not a castle, in a cattle stall, not a cathedral. This is not accidental. God intends that the movement begin with the grass roots. God intends the movement to begin in a humble way, not hierarchically.

The movement begins with Mary and Joseph making their journey to a small town called Bethlehem. The journey is almost improvisational, almost spontaneous—in hurried response to a decree by an emperor. They find themselves in a manger, giving birth to Jesus amid the smells of the hay and the soft noises of the animals, with the stars lighting the dark night, a remarkable Christmas Eve.

In the beginning, God wants us to know that the focus of the Christian movement is on the manger, not on the manager. The truth is this: the less organization, the more movement; the more organization, the less movement. It has taken me years of research and reflection, study and thought, to discover this profound, simple truth.

By nature and learning, I am a reasonably organized person. Julie will share with you how I count on a certain order, structure, and organization to be part of my life. Things have their place. My workbench is mostly well organized. My study is orderly. I know where each of my many books is; they are longtime friends, and each has its place. I am thus *into* being organized. Over the years, from countless family members and friends, I have learned, however, that what really counts are relationships of love and caring, not structure and organization.

In the Christian movement and in healthy local congregations, what counts is that we have just enough organization to advance the movement, but not so much organization that we harm the movement. Nor do we want so much organization that the organization becomes the focus of the movement, or worse yet, the organization *becomes* the movement.

Some movements continue as movements. Some movements become institutions. This progression from movement to institution usually begins when, innocently enough, someone says, "We need to get better organized." Then a progression typically happens:

- The movement begins, with the originating spirit and power of the movement

- The movement continues, plus some organization is now added
- The movement continues, with a stronger focus now primarily on organization
- The movement now becomes the organization, *with the originating spirit of the movement now subsumed under the need to protect, preserve, and perpetuate the organization*

Residually, faintly, like the whispering remnant of a cool breeze, the originating spirit may still be present, but the focus has now become the organized structure.

For some, their feeling, their desire for a stricter, more detailed organization may be driven by their compulsion toward perfectionism. For others, the sentiment for being organized springs from their need, their drive for power and control. They see "getting organized" as their way to power. Some may be less comfortable in a flexible movement. They want the structural comfort of an organization; they like things to be tidy and well ordered. They do not like any hint of chaos. For many people, it could be that they want to be helpful, but they are really too helpful. Their compulsion toward helpfulness, or sometimes their desire for helpful control, results in more organization than is useful to the movement.

There was a day when Jesus found himself visiting with the mother of two brothers. She wanted Him to do her a favor. Two of her sons were His close followers, two of His disciples. She wanted Jesus to arrange for one to sit at His right hand and the other to sit at His left hand. Her assumption was that some form of organization would be needed in this movement. Her further assumption was that this organization would be hierarchical in orientation, and she wanted both of her sons to be on top.

A movement is a matter of spirit, not size. A movement is a matter of spirit, not organization. What marks a movement is the spirit of its mission, not the details of its organization. We want just enough organization to be helpful, but not so much organization that the organization becomes harmful and creates a codependent-dependent pattern of behavior between the organization and the movement.

In the course of human history, we have seen these possibilities:

1. Some movements begin as a movement and continue as a movement.

2. Some movements begin as a movement and become an institution, and it works, so long as it is in a time of institutions.

3. Some institutions begin as an institution, and it works, so long as it is in a time of institutions.

4. Some institutions begin as an institution, and when it is a time of movements they learn how to be a movement. They flourish.

5. Some movements begin as a movement and become an institution, but it does not work when it is a time of movements. They wither.

6. Some movements begin as a movement and become an institution in a time of institutions, and when it is a time of movements, they relearn how to be a movement. They flourish.

Consider which of these possibilities you and your congregation are living out. You can consider which contributes to your being a strong, healthy congregation in this time.

A movement is like a jazz-improvisational group. It is like a hammered dulcimer jam session, like a fast break down the basketball court. A movement is like a spur-of-the-moment gathering of friends and family—a sharing of God's grace, a discovering of God's hope. It is not like a carefully planned, formal, sit-down dinner requiring weeks of tedious, detailed organization and preparation. It is a warm, informal gathering of gentle laughter, shared hopes, and a sense of the presence of the grace of God.

A movement is like a sailing ship, beautiful and nimble, tacking now this way and that, playing to the best of the winds as it heads toward its destination. A movement is like the moment of a sunrise, bringing new life and new hope. We have this confidence and assurance: the sunrise comes each dawn, bringing a new day of possibilities and promise.

God's Gift of the Present

This book confirms the possibilities God has now given to us. For a long time, I thought of these as emerging trends; then I discovered these trends have already happened. The future has come, and the future that has happened includes these possibilities for reaching and growing the grass roots of your congregation:

- Movement more than institution
- Compassion more than commitment
- Stars more than this planet
- Sprinter more than marathon runner
- Grassroots mission more than top-down maintenance
- Creativity more than control
- Whole more than the parts

We are richly blessed with these new possibilities. They are the reality that has happened. God gives them to us in the present. They have come to pass. Consider which of these are actively alive in you. Think of which of the possibilities you can advance and develop, build and grow in your congregation. Decide which of these you will have fun expanding and adding, so that these realities are lived out, richly, fully, in your life and in the life of your congregation.

There is singular truth in the old saying, "Yesterday was history. Tomorrow is a mystery. Today is a gift. That is why it is called the present." There is truth in this. Yesterday is but a dream and tomorrow is only a vision. But today, well lived, makes every yesterday a dream of happiness and every tomorrow a vision of hope. Look well, therefore, to this day.

I frequently say, "We look to the future, so we know what to do in the present. The purpose of long-range planning is to know what to do today, not so we know what to do tomorrow. We set the date for the wedding; then we work backward from that date. Once we know the date for the wedding, we know what it makes sense to do today."

God gives us our future *in our present.* We can only live in the present. Thus, God brings our future to us now and lets us live our future now . . . in the present. The future has come. The future has happened.

We talk of the past, present, and future.

The past is the present of an earlier time. We remember that earlier present. We are shaped and shape ourselves by our memories of that earlier present. But the past has reality only as *an earlier present.* It was not "the past" when it happened. Indeed, at that time, it "happens," not "happened." We may look back reflectively, but at the time it happened it was our present.

Finally, there is no past, only the memories we have in the present. Our memories of the past live in the present, the past that is forgiven and celebrated, forgotten and remembered. But the past no longer exists, except in the present.

The future can only live in the present. The future is not something out there that has reality in the future. Yes, God goes before us as a cloud by day and a fire by night, leading us to the future God is promising and preparing for us, and God does so in the present.

Finally, there is no future, only our expectancy in the present, only our anticipation and anxiety, hope and dread, trust and tribulation, faith and fear that what is coming indeed has come, will advance the present. The future does not yet exist, and when it does, it will exist only as the present. The future can happen only in the present. Indeed, the future has happened now. *We cannot live in the past or the future. We can live only in the present.*

Some try to live in the past. They are lonely. Some try to live in the future. They are frustrated. One can only live in this present moment, hoping that the coming present moment will be new and fresh, healthy and advancing. Finally, there is only the present. God blesses us with this gift: the future has come. You can choose to live in the future that has come. You will live a whole, healthy life. You can help your congregation do the same. You will have a strong, healthy congregation. You will reach and grow the grass roots.

Regrettably, some choose the past that has been. They decide to live there. They do not reach the grass roots. They grow older and grayer, fewer and weaker as the days and months pass. For them, the memories of the past become the present in which they live. I wish they could choose otherwise. I honor their decision. They have the right to decide the life they plan to live. They are aware of the consequences of their decision. They know they will be older and grayer, fewer and weaker. They know their congregation will be weak and declining, then dying, then finally dead. No amount of cajoling or threatening will change their minds. That is fine. It is their choice. I wish them well. I understand.

Fortunately, God gives us the choice. I encourage you to decide well. I encourage you to have confidence and assurance in your present. God gives you seven possibilities with which to reach and grow the grass roots, to live a whole, healthy life, to be a strong, healthy congregation.

The Future That Has Come	*The Past That Has Been*
Possibilities for reaching and growing the grass roots	Ways not to reach and grow the grass roots
Movement	Institution
Compassion	Commitment
Stars	Planet
Excellent sprinter	Solid marathon runner
Mission	Maintenance
Creativity	Control
Focus on the whole of life	Focus on part of life

We are the Christian movement. We began in a manger. We grow in our understanding through the life and teachings of Jesus. We deepen our grasp of who we are with the events of Palm Sunday, the Upper Room, and Golgotha. We discover who we are with the open tomb, the risen Lord, and new life in Christ. With Pentecost, we come into our own.

We are the Christmas people, the people of wonder and joy. We are the people of the cross, the people of sacrifice and compassion. We are the Easter people, the people of new life and hope. We are the people of Pentecost, the people of service and mission.

We began as a movement, not an institution. Institutions will still be with us. They continue to do the work they can do. Mostly, they do it as well as they can. There may come a day—in the distant future—when institutions once again have compelling value with the grass roots, but not today. This is the day of movements.

The future of the Christian movement is in reaching and growing the grass roots. There is no future without the grass roots. In our time, the Christian movement cannot move forward in a top-down, bureaucratic, organizational, institutional manner. Many have tried that route. It has not worked.

This is a time for movements, not institutions. This is a time for us to return to our roots. This is a time to return to how we began. This is a time to return to the manger and the open tomb. This is a time for us, with the grace of God, the compassion of Christ, and the hope of the Holy Spirit, to be, richly and fully, the Christian movement. The way forward is reaching and growing the grass roots. The way forward is not to focus on the past that has been. The way forward is to focus on the future that has come.

2

Motivations, Grass Roots, Key Leaders

But while he was yet at a distance, his father saw him, and had compassion, and ran and embraced him. . . .

—LUKE 15:20

We met in high school. I can see her now, sitting in the front row near the teacher's desk. Mr. Heinz presided over the third floor study hall, in room 302. He was the speech and drama teacher. With a senatorial voice, gray hair, tall of stature, a quiet spirit, and a commanding presence, he served as coach of the varsity debate team and advisor to the drama club.

My study hall was on the second floor, in room 201. I was a senior that year, which had its privileges. I was on the varsity debate team. Jim Coleman and I were partners. Jim was a grand partner. We balanced one another with our debating strengths. Together, we were an excellent match. We did well that year. We were the affirmative team, and we won many debates against major competition. It was an extraordinary year.

During the course of the year, I would get a hall pass to go from my study hall to Mr. Heinz's study hall. He and I would discuss strategies for the upcoming debate tournaments. It was especially useful preparation for the coming Saturday debates.

Julie and I came to know one another. She was a sophomore. Sitting near Mr. Heinz's desk gave us the opportunity to visit. She is a generous person, with a spirit of confidence and assurance, openness and graciousness. We would talk, particularly on those occasions when Mr. Heinz had to run an errand and left me in charge of the study hall.

Julie and I became good friends. We had our first date, a square dance at her church. We had a good time. More dates followed. As I came to know her better, I discovered, increasingly, her quiet, gentle ways of sharing compassion with those around her.

We fell in love. Time passed. We married.

We celebrate many wonderful years of married life together. Two excellent sons have been born to us. They are gifts of God. They have emerged as solid human beings. We are proud to be their parents. Three grandchildren bless our lives.

We celebrate many remarkable years of ministry together. We began serving as associate minister of a congregation, while studying at the university. It was an amazing time, sharing with hardworking people. Mostly, they were employed in the nearby tire factories of Akron.

We lived on the third floor of the Wesley Foundation and looked after the building. Rev. Bill Van Valkenburg was the director. He was an immense encouragement and a generous friend. During this time, we also served the Mountville and Thompson congregations, while their pastor was on an extended leave.

Then we were the first pastoral couple actually to live in Brady Lake. The sign said Brady Lake Community Church. They arranged with the district superintendent to have a pastor. Prior to our coming, once a month or sometimes once a week, a pastor would drive out to Brady Lake to preach on Sunday.

The year we went to Brady Lake, there was no parsonage. We lived that summer with Mrs. Ida Mae Stratton in her big, old farmhouse. Her husband had died that spring. She had room. We would be company with her. We had a grand time sharing and living together. Her strawberry patch was right outside her kitchen door. Each evening we would have strawberries for dessert.

In the fall, a small cottage was found down on the lake. It was for rent. It would work well. Living catty-corner across the lane from us were Orville and Mary Hissom. Big, warm, wise Orville was the principal of the school and mentor of the community. We learned much from him. Mary was cheerful, with a sense of joy in her life. She was a nurse, and when later our first son was born, she was a wonderful help to us.

Harold and Wilma Dodds lived two houses down from us, right across from the Hissoms. Harold had a good spirit and practical common sense, and he could fix most anything. Wilma shared the warmth of her happiness, her humor, and her tender ways.

They and the Hissoms were close, good friends. The four of them were generous to include us and to love us, warmly and fully. Many an evening, we sat together on the Dodds's front porch, our laughter floating out across the lake, sharing with one another, talking of family, reflecting on life and its course. These were good friends and good times. During our time at Brady Lake, we—meaning the congregation, with much volunteer labor—built a parsonage, which has helped the community to have a pastor ever since.

In the years that have come and gone, Julie and I have had the privilege of serving congregations in Ohio, Texas, and Georgia. We share our gratitude with the people of Goodyear Heights, Mountville, Thompson, Brady Lake, Lovers Lane, Pleasant Valley, Bethel, Mt. Gilead, Turin, and Coke's Chapel. We have learned much from them and their compassion.

We have spoken to countless seminars; workshops; and regional, national, and international events. We have had the privilege of helping thousands upon thousands of key leaders and ministers. We have traveled afar. We have served as consultants with thousands of congregations, helping them develop a strong, healthy future in God's mission.

We have had the honor of teaching for many years at one of the strongest seminaries on the planet. We have taught, shared with, and learned from thousands of students who are now serving God's mission in extraordinary ways.

The books we have written have a life of their own. They travel around the globe, benefiting people in this country, Canada, England, Australia, New Zealand, and beyond. Translated into various languages, they are used in Korea, a number of countries in Africa, the Caribbean, Latvia, Austria, Russia, and nations in Central and South America.

We share many remarkable years of marriage and ministry. We look forward to the years to come, and the ways in which we can best serve God's mission. In each place we have lived, Julie has shared her compassion—with children in the neighborhood, people in the hospital, individuals in need, with her family, and with her colleagues at work.

God's greatest gift to me is, finally, not the congregations served, students helped, courses taught, seminars led, lectures delivered, national and international events spoken to, or the churches strengthened with my consultation. Nor is it the books written, translated, and used around the world. These are remarkable gifts, given of God. Yet they pale compared to God's primary gift to me. If I could be known for anything, it would not be for these things.

God's greatest gift is to be "Julie's husband." In the area of the Rocky Mountains where we like to spend much of our free time, Julie is known widely for her contributions in several groups, especially in the quilting group. This is among the strongest groups in the region. With my speaking and travel schedule, she is there more than I am. She is better known there than I am. When I meet someone in the area for the first time, the person says, with considerable delight and enthusiasm, "Oh, you're Julie's husband!" To be Julie's husband is the deepest, richest honor in this life's journey.

Late one night as I was writing this chapter, these words came to me.

Intelligent and wise
Gentle and soft
A star in her eyes
She saw the future before I did

A wonderful surprise
The path we have followed
Is more than I could dream
The wonder of it all
Is hers to glean

Hope is life
Hope is my wife
Love is life
Love is my wife . . . Julie

God blesses us with people with whom we discover the full meaning of compassion. I am grateful for the countless mentors and friends whom God has given to me, and who have shared and now share their compassion with me. I have discovered much about compassion through the grace of God, the compassion of Christ, and the hope of the Holy Spirit.

I am especially grateful for all I have learned and am discovering about compassion from Julie McCoy Callahan. God sends special people to each of us. I am thankful God sent Julie to me. Her sense of generosity, her gentle sharing with people, her deep love for people, her sense of forgiveness, generous and full—all these help me understand the richness, the fullness of compassion.

Motivational Resources

There is a time for compassion. There is a time for commitment. This is the time for compassion. In this new time, we have seen a major paradigm shift from commitment to compassion. A healthy congregation lives with compassion. Its members have the confidence and assurance that one compelling way of reaching and growing the grass roots is thinking and planning, behaving, and living with the motivation of compassion. In a larger sense, in this new time, they share these three major motivations: compassion, community, and hope.

In an earlier time, a congregation could focus primarily on the motivations of challenge, reasonability, and commitment. In our time, compassion, community, and hope are more encouraging than challenge, reasonability, and commitment. Challenge, reasonability, and commitment are encouraging. Compassion, community, and hope are more encouraging. A strong, effective congregation shares the motivations of compassion, community, and hope more than the motivations of challenge, reasonability, and commitment. The first three are its majors. The second three are the minors.

Motivation is internal, not external. All six of these motivational resources—compassion, community, hope, challenge, reasonability, and commitment—are present within each of us. God blesses us with these resources. We draw on them. We motivate ourselves with them. They lead us to God; help us live whole, healthy lives; and help us serve well in the Christian movement.

We can develop whichever of the six we would have fun growing. At the same time, in day-to-day life, one motivational resource—or more frequently two—come to be predominant. They tend to be the two that with some consistency we have a propensity to head toward, as we motivate ourselves. For a given time in our lives, these two are the two we have learned to depend on. Life is a pilgrimage. Life is a journey. It is not the same two for all of one's life. We are not locked in to the same two forever. For now, for this time of life, there will be two specific motivations that predominate. Later, it may be yet another two. We learn and grow. We advance and develop.

In a congregation, all six motivational resources are present in the key leaders and the pastor. Two tend to be predominant. All six are present with the grass roots of the congregation and the unchurched in the community. The hook, the catch, is that it is not always the same two motivations. On the one hand, the key leaders and pastor may motivate themselves with a certain two. On the other hand, the grass roots and unchurched may motivate themselves with two others. This mismatch is particularly the case in a weak, declining, or dying congregation.

Compassion is sharing, caring, giving, loving, and serving. Compassion is forgiving and reconciling. Compassion is fairness, equity, and justice. Compassion is hard and tough, not soft and easy. Compassion is generous without leading to codependency. Compassion includes the giving and accepting of forgiveness. Many people motivate themselves out of their spirit of compassion, and many acts of compassion have a spirit of quiet generosity about them.

Community is good fun and good times. Community is roots, place, and belonging. Community is friends and family. Many of us motivate ourselves out of a spirit of community. We long for, yearn for, a sense of belonging and family. This is especially so as the extended family clans that used to deliver this are now, for the most part, scattered asunder across the landscape. We feel like strangers, aliens in a foreign land. We seek a new sense of home.

Hope is the confidence and assurance that God's grace is with us, that the compassion of Christ sustains us, and that the hope of the Holy Spirit leads us in this present day and in the days to come. We look for sources of hope in the present and in the immediate future. When we cannot find them there, we look for sources of hope in the distant future. We even look for sources of hope in the next-life future beyond the river. We project our hopes down the road.

We mostly long for and look for signs of hope in the present. Our search for spirituality is our search for hope. Our search for the Holy One is our search for hope. Our search for transcendence is our search for hope. We count on and look forward to the confidence and assurance that some of our deepest yearnings and longings will be fulfilled in the hope and grace of God.

Challenge is the drive, the quest, toward attainment, accomplishment, and achievement. Some people rise to the bait of a challenge; to them, a primary internal motivational resource is the goal of attainment, the challenge of accomplishment, and the result of achievement. They look forward to this project and then to the next one. For them, life is one intriguing challenge after another.

Reasonability is the search for data, analysis, logic, "it makes good sense." I work with congregations in Silicon Valley that have a high density of engineers, scientists, and data-processing experts. Reasonability is a major motivation for them. I work with congregations in small college towns with a high density of professorial members. Logic and analysis are important motivations for them.

I worked with one church that had been "burned" seventeen years in a row. I do not mean the building went up in flames seventeen times. They tried something new each year for seventeen years. None of the things they tried worked. They got burned. Reasonability became a major motivation: "It had better make reasonable sense," the people in this church say, "before we stick our hand in the flame the eighteenth time."

I honor this fact. I have never yet met anyone who got married out of the motivation of reasonability. Most people get married out of the motivations of compassion and community, and then they rationalize why it made better sense to get married early, rather than wait until later.

Commitment is a primary motivational resource for many people. Commitment is duty, vows, obligation, and loyalty. A vast number of people have the notion that if they are loyal to the company the company will be loyal to them. They make deep, abiding commitments to their company, to their family, and to their church.

All six motivational resources are present in each of us. Two tend to predominate. This is what I call the multiple motivation theory of behavior. In life, we tend to motivate ourselves forward based on two, sometimes more, of these primary motivational resources. To be sure, sometimes, one motivation results in behavior. Most times, it takes two or more of these motivational resources to move behavior forward.

Our older son, Ken—excellent son—has two predominant motivational resources: compassion and challenge. Both the culture and his parents taught him that one of the best motivational resources that a first-born son has is the motivation of challenge. He rises to a challenge. It is therefore not accidental that at a comparatively young age he is one of the leaders of a corporation that is prominent in this country and abroad.

Our younger son—excellent son—started life learning to get along with three other family members, his older brother, his mother, and his father. In a way, he is the only one who ever had to learn how to get along with the three other people in the family.

His two predominant motivational resources are compassion and community. He chooses a job as much for the people he will be working with as for the challenge of the post. Some few years ago, working for an international hotel chain, Mike's restaurant team placed number one in the whole chain. When the photographer came to take the picture, Mike wanted the picture to include the whole team, not just him.

It took our younger son seventeen years to teach me that he could not be motivated by the challenge of homework ("Why can't you be like your older brother and see the challenge in this homework?"). Mike wrote his best term papers as he and two good friends gathered in an upstairs bedroom. Below, we wondered whether they were working on a term paper or having a party. That's called community.

One of the fatal mistakes some of us make is to assume that because we motivate ourselves in a certain way, we can help other people motivate themselves in the same way that we motivate ourselves. It is a fatal mistake. The art is to discover which two, among these six motivational resources, are primary for them. Then encourage them to motivate themselves in keeping with the resources that work best for them. People motivate themselves in the ways that work for them.

Now, I do honor that there are demotivators in life. Some of these are anxiety, fear, anger, rage, analysis paralysis, jealousy, despair, despondency, depression, and greed. We could develop an even longer list of the demotivators that distract us from the healthy motivations with which God blesses us. On occasion, we may find ourselves doing something out of one of these demotivators. Frequently, anxiety leads to fear,

fear to anger, and anger to rage. Despair, despondency, depression seem to go together. I call these demotivators because they lead us to our lesser selves. They seldom lead to constructive behavior.

The six motivational resources advance whole, healthy, constructive behavior in our lives. There may be other constructive motivational resources besides these six. Over the years, in my research and interviews, and in small and large group discussions, people have taught me that these six are the ones on which they most often draw to live whole, healthy lives. In my study of the Old and New Testaments, I discover these six as being the ones with which God blesses us and with which God encourages us. In this time, among the six, compassion, community, and hope help congregations in reaching and growing the grass roots.

Match and Gap

A strong, healthy congregation develops a motivational match between the key leaders and the grass roots, the pastor and the unchurched. A weak, declining congregation creates a motivational gap. A dying congregation makes the motivational gap wider.

Any two of the first three resources—compassion, community, and hope—are a motivational match. What you can count on and depend upon is that the grass roots and the unchurched live on the motivational resources of compassion, community, and hope. Whenever the key leaders, grass roots, pastor, staff, and unchurched resonate on any two of these first three, a motivational match is created. The congregation is healthy and effective, serving well in God's mission.

It could be a motivational match based on compassion and community.

Motivational Match Based on Compassion and Community

	KEY LEADERS	GRASS ROOTS	PASTOR AND STAFF	UNCHURCHED
Compassion	•	•	•	•
Community	•	•	•	•
Hope				
Challenge				
Reasonability				
Commitment				

It could be a motivational match based on compassion and hope.

Motivational Match Based on Compassion and Hope

	KEY LEADERS	GRASS ROOTS	PASTOR AND STAFF	UNCHURCHED
Compassion	•	•	•	•
Community				
Hope	•	•	•	•
Challenge				
Reasonability				
Commitment				

It could be a motivational match based on community and hope.

Motivational Match Based on Community and Hope

	KEY LEADERS	GRASS ROOTS	PASTOR AND STAFF	UNCHURCHED
Compassion				
Community	•	•	•	•
Hope	•	•	•	•
Challenge				
Reasonability				
Commitment				

Regrettably, some congregations create for themselves a motivational gap. Whenever the key leaders, the pastor, and the staff focus on any two of these—challenge, reasonability, commitment—they create, for their congregation, a motivational gap. The congregation becomes weak and declining. The more insistent the key leaders and the pastor are on any two of the second set of three, the wider the motivational gap and the more likely it is that the congregation is dying.

In a weak, declining congregation, a typical pattern is for the key leaders and the pastor to focus on the motivations of challenge and commitment, while the grass roots and the unchurched live on the motivations of compassion and community. There is no resonance. There is no match. There is a motivational gap.

Motivational Gap

	KEY LEADERS	GRASS ROOTS	PASTOR AND STAFF	UNCHURCHED
Compassion		•		•
Community		•		•
Hope				
Challenge	•		•	
Reasonability				
Commitment	•		•	

The more the key leaders and the pastor—in a retrenching, retreating posture—seek to reinforce commitment and challenge, the wider the motivational gap. Increasingly, the congregation moves from weak and declining to dying. The congregation dies because a few deeply committed, high-challenge leaders and the pastor work very hard on the wrong motivations.

The same can be said for challenge and reasonability, or reasonability and commitment. In all instances, what the key leaders and the pastor create is a motivational gap. The result is that fewer and fewer people do most of the work and give most of the money. The weak, declining congregation becomes a dying congregation. The key leaders and the pastor do not understand why this has happened. They rise to the challenge and deepen their commitment. They work even harder. As they do so, the motivational gap becomes wider and wider. They decline. They die.

In some instances, people have misapplied the "20–80" action principle to excuse the dilemma of weak, declining, and dying congregations. The 20–80 principle is simply this:

- Twenty percent of what a group does delivers 80 percent of its results, accomplishments, and achievements.
- Eighty percent of what a group does delivers 20 percent of its results, accomplishments, and achievements.

Vilfredo Pareto is the individual who researched and developed this principle. It has been widely used and is widely helpful.

Regrettably, some have misapplied this principle, inappropriately and inaccurately, to the behavior of weak, declining, and dying congregations. In their misapplication, some suggest that 20 percent of the people do 80 percent of the work and give 80 percent of the money. They go on to suggest that 80 percent of the people do 20 percent of the work and give 20 percent of the money. Pareto never meant either of those misapplications. Whenever we find a few people doing most of the work and giving most of the money, we have not found the 20–80 principle.

What we have found is a motivational gap.

Again and again, the key leaders and the pastors say, in committee meeting after committee meeting, "If people were only more committed and could see the challenge, this blooming venture would get better." They motivate themselves on the motivational wavelengths of challenge and commitment. They broadcast to the grass roots and the unchurched—they seek to motivate the grass roots and the unchurched—on the motivational wavelengths of challenge and commitment. However, the grass roots and the unchurched have their radios tuned to the motivational wavelengths of compassion, community, and hope. The broadcast from the key leaders and the pastor comes through to them as just so much static.

Think about these motivational resources as radio wavelength signals. In an effective, healthy congregation, the key leaders and the pastor broadcast on the motivational wavelength frequencies of compassion, community, and hope. This resonates with the grass roots and the unchurched. That is where they have their radios tuned. Because of this motivational match, many people help with the work and many people give generously.

By contrast, the key leaders and the pastor in a weak and declining or dying congregation broadcast on the frequencies of challenge, reasonability, and commitment. It does not resonate. Thus, a few people end up doing most of the work and giving most of the money.

Reaching and growing the grass roots means reaching them through the motivational resources by which they motivate themselves, not by the motivational resources by which we motivate ourselves. A regrettable assumption is that because we motivate ourselves based on challenge, reasonability, and commitment, we can therefore motivate them, or they will motivate themselves, on the same wavelengths of challenge, reasonability, and commitment. It is a fatal mistake. The art is to respect how people motivate themselves and encourage them to use the motivational resources that work well for them.

For example, when inviting Mary to teach Sunday school, I encourage people to say, "Mary, we invite you to come and fall in love with this group of kids and give them the privilege of falling in love with you." It is an invitation of compassion and community.

So Mary comes and falls in love with the group of kids and the kids with her, and they bring their friends to that legendary Sunday school class. Kids care what the teacher knows, when they know the teacher cares. The foundation of learning is love. Another way I say this principle is "the team plays well for the coach who loves the team."

What I would not say to Mary is, "Mary, would you be willing to teach this certain Sunday school class this coming year?" That is an invitation to commitment. People live forward or downward in response to our invitations with them. Regrettably, Mary will come, do her duty, take her turn, fulfill her commitment, and likely never fall in love with that group of kids. I learned this in interviews I have done. Twenty and thirty years later, I ask someone, "In addition to your parents, who meant the most to you during your growing-up years?" Over and over, I hear the name of a Sunday school teacher. What happened is the teacher fell in love with them and they fell in love with the teacher.

Another example. People say to me again and again, "Dr. Callahan, help us find a pastor who will come and love us and whom we can come to love." I almost never hear from the grass roots of the congregation, "Help us find a pastor who is a high-challenge type, deeply committed, and with a focus on reasonability." I do hear that from key leaders, but almost never from the grass roots.

Another example. A congregation is doing its annual giving and stewardship campaign. They are halfway through their campaign. The congregation has two hundred households. What we know is that the first one hundred households will pledge and give $100,000. What we also know is that we will be lucky if the second one hundred households pledge and give $20,000. Everyone knows these statistical analyses. It is, however, one thing to know the analysis, and it is another thing to understand why it happens.

Regrettably, key leaders who are deeply committed with a sense of high challenge plan many campaigns. They have Loyalty Sundays, commitment cards, and challenge thermometer goals. There is a high density of key leaders in the first one hundred households. The motivations of commitment and challenge resonate with them. The result is that they respond generously.

In planning the current year's giving and stewardship campaign, the leaders remember that in recent years they did not do as well with the second hundred households. Moreover, although they do not actually raise their voices, there is a sense in which they do intensify the decibel emphasis on commitment and challenge. If it was ten decibels with the first hundred households, with the second hundred households it is forty decibels of commitment and challenge. They remind the grassroots households of their membership vows. The appeal is to commitment. They tell them how difficult things will be if they do not live up to their vows. They ask them to see the challenge.

They create a motivational gap. There is no resonance. There is no match. Thus with the second hundred households what they actually raise is passive-aggressive behavior, low-grade hostility, subliminal resentment, and eruptive forms of anger—and $20,000.

What the grassroots households do is give their other $80,000 to those groupings that stir their compassion and touch their sense of community. It is not that they do not give. They give with generosity. They simply do not give to those causes that do not match their motivations for giving. They give to the causes that touch their sense of compassion and community. Further, during each stewardship campaign, they learn that the key leaders of the congregation do not value, respect, and honor the motivations out of which they, as grassroots people, give. They learn that the key leaders quietly insist that their motivations as key leaders should be the motivations out of which the grass roots should give.

We could have a giving and stewardship campaign built on the motivations of compassion and community. We could have a Love Sunday, not a Loyalty Sunday. We could have a mission budget, not a maintenance budget. We could have a People Served in Mission goal rather than a challenge thermometer goal. We could have a Compassion Card, not a Commitment Card. Who invented a Commitment Card? Someone motivated by commitment.

The Compassion Card could say something like, "We are grateful for the compassion and generosity of God's gifts in our lives. We generously pledge and look forward to giving (fill in the blank) to advance God's mission in the coming year." We will discover that the grassroots households, the second hundred households, give as generously as the first hundred households do.

I recall someone talking about the radio preacher who airs every Saturday afternoon in their town, whose sermons on commitment are so strident that they could pulverize concrete. He shared how this radio preacher, in a dull, deadly, boring sermon, hammers, hammers, hammers again and again at commitment. This person talked about how he can stand on a street corner in that town any Saturday afternoon at four o'clock, watching people drive by in their cars, and know the ones who are listening to that radio preacher as they slump lower and lower behind the wheel of their car.

Jesus did not say to Peter, "Peter, will you rise to the challenge, will you make the commitment?" What Jesus said to Peter is, "Peter, do you love me?" "Yes, Lord." "Peter, feed my sheep." Jesus invites Peter's motivations of compassion and community.

The text in I Corinthians 13 does not say, "Now abide challenge, reasonability, and commitment, and the greatest of these is commitment." What the text says is, "Now abide faith, hope, and compassion, and the greatest of these is compassion."

Francis of Assisi said it well: "Go and preach the Gospel. Use words, if necessary." The early vows of the Christian movement were:

Do you love the Lord, your God, with all your heart and mind and soul and strength?

Do you love Christ as your Lord and Savior?

Will you love your neighbor as generously as you love yourself?

Will you live a life of compassion, community, and hope?

The text does not say, "For God was so challenged by the world . . ." God may very well be challenged by the mess we are making of God's world, but what the text says is that "God so loved the world." Jesus invites people: "Love your neighbor." Yes, discipleship is compassion.

A Time for Compassion

There is a time for compassion. There is a time for commitment. This is the time for compassion. In a time of institutions, the motivations of challenge, commitment, and reasonability seem at home. The phrase "Be loyal to the company and the company will be loyal to you" seems to work more fully in an institutional time. In a time of movements, the motivational resources of compassion, community, and hope thrive and flourish—have compelling value.

The day of commitment is over. The day of compassion has come. The day of law is over. The day of grace has come. God invites us to our deepest compassion, strongest love, and most generous mercy. God invites us to build motivational matches between key leaders, grassroots members, pastors, and the unchurched on any two of these three: compassion, community, hope.

Now, I am not knocking challenge, reasonability, and commitment. Specifically, I am not knocking commitment. The list could look like this:

- Compassion
- Community
- Hope
- Challenge
- Reasonability

I could quit there. I am for commitment. It made the list. What I am confirming is this: welcome to the first century; welcome to the twenty-first century. Welcome to a time of new beginnings.

It took the Christian movement one thousand nine hundred plus years to create institutional, organizational, bureaucratic membership vows that sounded like, "Will you be loyal to such and such denomination and support it by your prayers, your presence, your gifts, and your service?"

In the first century, there were no such institutional membership vows, and there were no denominations to which to be loyal. What was at stake was, "Will you love the Lord, your God? Will you love Jesus Christ as your Lord and Savior? Will you love your neighbor as generously as you love yourself? Will you live a life of compassion, community, and hope in the Christian movement?" What was at stake were mission vows, not membership vows; movement vows, not institutional vows.

Some people say to me, "Dr. Callahan, what we need is people who can see the challenge of this place." I usually say to them, "Good Friend, you have just taught me you motivate yourself with challenge." I go on to say, "If there were lots of people out there who motivated themselves on challenge, we would do very well on challenge. What is out there, among the grass roots and unchurched, are people who motivate themselves on compassion, community, and hope."

Some people say to me, "Dr. Callahan, what we need is people who can see the reasonability of what we are about." I usually say to them, "Good Friend, you have just taught me you motivate yourself with reasonability. If there were lots of people out there who motivate themselves on reasonability, we would do very well on reasonability. What is out there, among the grass roots and the unchurched, are people who motivate themselves on compassion, community, and hope."

Many people say to me, "Dr. Callahan, what we need is people with more commitment." I usually say to them, "Good Friend, you have just taught me you are a long-time Christian."

The early motivations that bring all of us to the grace of God, the compassion of Christ, and the hope of the Holy Spirit are the motivations of compassion, community, and hope. That early song is not, "Yes, Jesus is committed to me." The early song is, "Yes, Jesus loves me." The song "Amazing Grace" does not speak of amazing challenge or amazing commitment; it speaks of the amazing love and grace of God.

What happens is that we are drawn to the Christian movement out of compassion, community, and hope. Then, after fifteen or twenty or thirty years of living in the Christian life, some people grow the motivation of commitment forward. Not all do, but some do—particularly key leaders. The consequence is that, for them, the important motivation that they believe everyone should have is the motivation of commitment.

I invite them to think about the people who, many years ago, helped them to become part of the Christian movement. They talk about the sense of compassion, the spirit of community, the abiding presence of hope in these people. I usually say to them, "What drew you, years ago, to the Christian movement were the qualities of compassion, community, and hope. How could you expect to draw in the grass roots and the unchurched with the motivations of challenge, reasonability, and commitment? That is not what drew you in. Why would it draw them? And that was a churched culture time; this is a mission field."

Although we were yet a long way off, God saw us, and had compassion and ran to us, and welcomed us home. God invites us to do the same with the unchurched. Not to wait until they get to the house. God did not wait on us. God ran to us. God invites us to put our arms around the unchurched, to share the same rich compassion God shares with us, and to welcome them home.

Discipleship is compassion. This is especially true for people new to the Christian movement. I honor the fact that discipleship is commitment. There are many books written on discipleship as commitment. Longtime Christians write them. The books simply teach us that commitment is a motivation among some people long in the Christian life. By itself, commitment is law, not grace. God invites us to grace. Compassion and commitment are good friends. The early motivations are compassion, community, and hope.

Someone says to me, "This is very insightful, very helpful, Dr. Callahan, but when do we get around to the tough one called commitment?"

I usually reply, "Good Friend, compassion is as tough as commitment. Think of the person who has harmed you, injured you, and grievously wronged you, against whom you have a grudge, bitterness, and deep-seated resentment. Sometime this week, with the grace of God, I invite you to forgive that person for the wrongs that they did to you.

"I don't necessarily suggest that you go and speak to that person. The art of making amends is to do no more harm than necessary. Inside yourself, with a spirit of compassion, forgive that person. I assure you that compassion is as tough as commitment, because compassion involves forgiveness. On the cross, Jesus said, 'Father, forgive them, for they know not what they do.' I assure you, compassion is as tough as commitment."

Indeed, all six motivational resources are tough. Living a life of compassion, community, hope, challenge, reasonability, or commitment is tough. Fortunately, God blesses us with these six motivational resources, and fortunately God helps us grow forward whichever of these six will help us live whole, healthy lives and serve well in God's mission.

I have the privilege of leading seminars with institutional church leaders around the globe. I have discovered that many denominational leaders immediately see the wisdom of developing motivational matches between key leaders, the pastor, the grass roots, and the unchurched.

Some few denominational leaders are reluctant to see the wisdom of doing so. They have based their recent lives heavily on challenge, reasonability, and commitment. In their frustration that these motivations do not work, they simply dig in and try harder to deepen their own commitment and rise to the greater challenge, hoping that people will see their example and motivate themselves the same way. The harder they try, the less it works. It worked well in the churched culture of thirty, and forty, and fifty years ago. Why not now?

This is a beginning time. This is a time for compassion, community, and hope. God blesses movements that live with the richness and fullness of these motivations.

3

Stars, Universe, and Beyond

Look toward heaven, and number the stars, if you are able to number them.

—GENESIS 15:5

We live in the stars. We used to live on this planet, looking out, or looking up, at the stars. Our frame of reference was this planet. When we thought of the "world," we thought of the Earth, or at most of our Milky Way. We now live in the midst of the stars. Our frame of reference is now the stars. We think of the world as this amazing, incredible universe we are in the process of discovering. In this new time, we have seen a major paradigm shift from this planet to the stars.

One possibility for reaching and growing the grass roots is to live as a movement, not an institution. A second is to share the motivations of compassion, community, and hope. A third possibility is to encourage people to make sense of living in this universe and on this planet rather than to ignore the discoveries of the universe that we are making. A healthy congregation, in this new time, helps people make sense of living in the stars. This congregation helps people develop a theology of the stars.

In an earlier time, congregations focused primarily on this planet. Our theology of the universe concentrated on Earth, our solar system, and it sometimes included the Milky Way. This is what we knew. We developed discernment about this limited world we knew. Now, making sense of living in the whole of God's universe is more helpful than ignoring the new discoveries of the universe. Focusing on this planet is helpful. Discovering the whole of God's universe is more helpful. There is a time for the stars. There is a time for the planet. This is the time for the stars.

Dulcinea and the Capodimonte Deep Field

"We are ready to transmit the contents of the disk."

The voice is warm, deep and clear, firm, expectant. The disk has been found on the fourth moon of the planet Santori in the twelfth galaxy from our sun. The planet was discovered in 2234 A.D. and named after the astronomer who first noted its existence. On closer examination, seven moons around the planet were found.

The signal from the disk was weak, mistaken for residual solar wind movement. Yet, the pattern of the signal was consistent. A landing craft was sent to search out the signal's source.

The landing party has found a video/audio disk of a make and design the space fleet has not used in more than one hundred years. The lab technicians, with help from an old database in the ship library, finally figure out how to download the disk. They are now ready to broadcast the video/audio disk to NASA in Houston and key leaders gathered in the White House.

The broadcast begins.

"This is Dulcinea Report 4. We have explored eleven galaxies, four star systems, and thirty-six planets. Long ago, we passed beyond the solar system of our earth. We went first to Andromeda, largely in tribute to and out of respect for the memory of Edwin Hubble. From Andromeda, we headed to Chepas 539 to explore the constellations in that part of our universe. From there, we went to Gabrielle 395.

"We are leaving a disk every so often along our journey. We have come too far from Earth to reach you with our communications system. We came up with the video/audio disk idea. We hope someone, later on, will find a disk and transmit our discoveries to Earth. This is the fourth disk we are leaving. We will leave others as we continue our explorations. This disk summarizes our progress to date.

"Our launch went well. The third space station made the difference. The first station, completed in 2007, 230 miles above Earth, and the moon station finished in 2035, would not have worked. Once the third space station was completed in 2055, 350 miles beyond the moon, launching from there greatly simplified our take-off power requirements. We made better time than we would have imagined to Andromeda.

"All systems are functioning at optimum. The ship is doing better than we anticipated. We are pleased with how well the Combination Propulsion System is operating.

"What follows is a summary of how we developed the ship and the results of our trip thus far. We thank the many people who have made this trip of a lifetime go so well.

"We have discovered that we have thirty-six remaining disks. We will leave a disk at significant points as we continue our explorations. We do not know whether any of the disks will be found. Moreover, we have been gone a long time. For those reasons, each disk will include the beginning research for our venture, how our ship is functioning, and how our journey is progressing. On each disk, we will summarize our earlier reports as well as our continuing progress to date.

"The first step in developing the Combined Propulsion System came from our years of sailing. Julie and I have sailed lakes in Ohio, Texas, and Georgia, off the Florida Keys, in the Bahamas, among the British Virgin Islands, and out of San Diego to the Pacific Ocean. The fuel that propels a sailboat is not on board the boat. It is in the wind outside the boat. As sailors, we are concerned as to whether there will be wind. There is no discussion of how to carry "propulsion fuel" on board a sailing ship. We talk about how to find the best wind patterns to propel the ship toward its destination.

"The second step came about as I read a research paper on the problem of carrying enough fuel to get anywhere in the galaxies. The paper detailed how to build a series of fuel depots, first in space, then on the moon, then on Mars, then on and on to establish supply bases for each step of exploration. The assumption: the fuel will have to be on board the ship. This assumption creates a problem. However massive the ship, it needs to carry much fuel on board as a major component of its size, weight, and bulk. The various fuel depots would keep the fuel components to a reasonable size for the next step on the journey.

"Time passed.

"The third step happened, late one October evening, as I was thinking of the power of the solar winds. It came to me that the solution to space travel was to draw on the variety of power sources in the universe rather than to carry power on board the ship.

"The fourth step came as I read, on the same day, seemingly by accident, two articles. One was a research paper on the Amazon River, some 4,195 miles long, flowing stronger than any other river in the world. About 3,300 miles of the river are more than five miles wide, in flood stage reaching sixty miles across. The Amazon, two hundred miles wide at its mouth, discharges sixty-four billion (64,000,000,000) gallons of fresh water per second. This discharge is so strong that it creates a "Gulf Stream" of fresh water that flows, as fresh water, two hundred miles out into the Atlantic Ocean.

"This reminded me of the Gulf Stream along the coast of the United States. Julie and I have sailed through this Gulf Stream many times. Although it is salt water, it nevertheless flows like a great river in the midst of the ocean from the Caribbean, up the East Coast of the United States, and across the Atlantic Ocean to Ireland and England.

"The other article was about neutrinos, small particles found throughout the universe. I began to wonder whether, amidst the neutrinos across the universe, there might be "rivers" of neutrinos that flow in certain directions.

"Our research led us to the discovery of nanoneutrinos, which indeed are like great Amazon rivers or Gulf Streams in the midst of the universe. We discovered that nanoneutrino oscillations induced by an eight-loop radiative mechanism created power. Now, we could sail the rivers of the galaxies.

"Much research followed. Finally, I identified these varied sources of power:

- The solar wind
- The rate and velocity of expansion in the universe
- The gravitational pull of various stars, planets, and black holes
- The radio and radar signals that are part of the universe
- The magnetic fields that appear in the universe
- The nanoneutrino rivers of the universe

"Excellent teams were gathered. In record time, we developed our solar wind power instrument. Much of the time, we simply "sail" with the solar winds.

"Next, we perfected the system that takes advantage of the rate and velocity of the expansion of the universe. This system "hooks onto" the momentum of the expanding universe. We have found it a useful source of power.

"Then we centered our research on the gravitational pull of various stars, planets, and black holes. Sometimes we allow the gravity of a given star to pull us forward.

"We built the propulsion system based on the radio and radar signals found across the universe. This is an effective source of power.

"This led us to develop the power system drawing on the magnetic fields that appear in the universe. Finally, we focused on the oscillation mechanism that discovers the nano-neutrino rivers flowing throughout the universe.

"We built a search-seek-and-store instrument that gathers power for our space ship. The device searches constantly for the various sources of power; seeks out the primary, nearest point of useful power; and stores sufficient supplies to provide instantaneous, on-demand power for our ship.

"Our miniaturized biocomputer assesses the multiple searches for available sources of power, interconnects the appropriate power instruments, and delivers the Combined Universal Power to our ship. We do not have to carry massive quantities of fuel on board our ship. We are like a sailboat. We tack our way across the galaxies, searching out, drawing on, and being propelled forward by the various power sources available in the universe.

"An excellent team gave leadership to building our space ship. Two large, barely known, recently discovered amoebae from the depths of the Pacific Ocean were "cultured." From them, an immense, virtually impervious amoeba emerged. Through a biografting procedure, the newest titanium, graphite, steel, and mytholedium skin became part of the amoeba. The result is a bioorganism, extraordinarily strong, that serves as our space ship. It can withstand enormous pressure, is highly flexible, and can adapt its shape to the power needs of the moment. If we need "sails" for solar winds, it can become that shape. If we need an elongated shape to take advantage of the gravitational pull of a distant planet, it can become that shape.

"Moreover, our ship lives on carbon dioxide and waste products from mammals. It gives off oxygen as a by-product. We developed three life support laboratories that meet our basic life needs through self-regenerating molecules of water, food, and air. The water has a wonderful taste and the food molecules are most nutritious. In addition to our self-regenerating molecule laboratories, we have a redundant system in that our ship produces oxygen as well. These dual systems make life easier on our ship. The air seems fresher and cleaner than on Earth.

"There is a remarkable symbiotic relationship between *Dulcinea* and us. We call the ship by that name because that is the name Julie and I gave our Coronado 25 sailboat, which we sailed in the Florida Keys and then for years on Lake Lanier. Dulcinea was the mythic princess for whom Don Quixote did his famous deeds. The team did excellent work in creating *Dulcinea*. She is a remarkable, flexible, livable ship.

"Last, we developed the force shield and weapons system. The force shield, at its standard setting, protects us from solar radiation. We were concerned that radiation would be a major problem. As it turns out, the force shield converts solar radiation into yet another source of power and energy for us. We have activated the double capacity of the force shield only once, as we navigated through a series of dense meteor showers. To date, we have found no use for our weapons system.

"Our communications module helped us stay in contact with Earth for a long time, functioning at a surprisingly extensive range, with a nanosecond response rate. We did not anticipate we would travel as fast as we have or come as far as we have.

"And so, here we are. We lost contact with Earth a long time ago. We now rely on the video/audio disks. Our library and instruments help us in our research of the universe. The power systems work better together than we expected. We have had to do very little "tacking" on our journey. We can usually find two or three power sources that help us stay our course in a reasonably straight line. We are making good time.

"I am including a copy of our ship's log, a number of pictures, and the data we have gathered to date about the galaxies, star systems, and planets we have explored. You will find the data helpful in planning future explorations in the stars. The universe is amazing. Know that we are safe. We wish you well. Thanks to all. Best to all. We are heading now to explore the Capodimonte Deep Field."

∞

There was silence in NASA. There was silence in the White House. *Dulcinea* had not been heard from for more than one hundred years. The date of the video/audio disk showed they had continued their explorations of the universe long after their last transmission. Did the bioorganic nature of their ship contribute to their living longer? Where, in the universe, were they now?

∞

B.H. and A.H.

The story of *Dulcinea* and the Capodimonte Deep Field could not have been written prior to January 1, 1925. Yes, before that date, there would have been stories about space. However, the space that humankind thought of was confined to this Milky Way. It is hard, given all the recent discoveries of the universe, to get back to that earlier time.

These days, in the normal course of playing, children refer to this star or that galaxy, this planet or that solar system. Children think in terms of living in the midst of the stars. They have never known a time when *Star Trek* was not. Children have a frame of reference that naturally includes the whole of the universe we are discovering. To move from this galaxy to that galaxy, from this constellation to that constellation, thousands of light years apart, is as natural as walking from one block in their neighborhood to the next. They are developing a theology of the stars.

Before January 1, 1925, humankind thought primarily of looking from the earth to the stars, and the stars were within our own Milky Way. The whole of the universe was our Milky Way.

For the Christian movement, the most decisive event in the course of humankind is the birth of Jesus of Nazareth. With great meaning and deep reverence, we think of human history as divided into B.C. and A.D. We measure the development of humankind in the light of the birth, life, teachings, death, and resurrection of Jesus Christ, the Risen Lord, and our Savior. Other remarkable events, although they are secondary, have happened in the course of human history. Among these is the extraordinary event that took place on January 1, 1925. Sometimes, I refer to everything before that date as B.H. (before Hubble), and everything after that date as A.H.

In an earlier time, our part of humanity thought of the world as the Mediterranean Basin. The people of the "Far East" thought, from their side of the planet, in a comparable way. (To them, we were probably the "Far West.") We were also aware of some peoples south of us in what we now think of as Africa and some, more fully after Alexander, to the southeast in what we now think of as India. We also had some contact with strange peoples to the north, in what is now Europe.

Our universe consisted of the Mediterranean Basin and the stars overhead. Our view was that the earth was the center of the universe. Then, as we learned more, we gave up that view, but we thought surely that our sun was the center of the universe. Then we gave up that view and came to the notion that definitely our solar system was the center of the universe. Finally, in the late 1800s and early 1900s we gave up that view and came to the conclusion that our Milky Way is the whole of the universe, and that Earth is part of it. By the turn of the twentieth century, the vast majority of astronomers agreed: the Milky Way was all there is. They held fast to the view that the Milky Way was the totality of the universe. There was nothing beyond. Indeed, it was inconceivable to think of "beyond."

In *Natural History,* dated December 1999-January 2000, in an article entitled "Beyond the Milky Way," in the Celestial Reports section, Richard Panek stated well the significance of January 1, 1925:

> On January 1, 1925, Edwin Hubble made public his finding that at least one "island universe" or galaxy of stars lies outside our own Milky Way. Throughout the nineteenth century, astronomers had debated the nature of nebulae— smudges of light at the farthest limits of telescopic sight, many of them in the shape of spirals.

Hubble's discovery made clear that the fuzzy patches were not part of our galaxy. He opened the door to the question of whether the Milky Way was the universe in its entirety. The possibility emerged that these nebulae were vast star systems entirely separate from, yet equal in magnitude to, our own galaxy.

In October 1923, Hubble found conclusive evidence to support his hypothesis regarding spiral nebulae as being distinct from our own Milky Way. He did so using the Mount Wilson telescope, at 100 inches then the most powerful astronomical mechanism invented by humankind. Focused on the Andromeda Nebula, Hubble detected a Cepheid variable, a star whose regular periods of brightening and fading correspond to its absolute magnitude. Such a star is useful in measuring galactic distances. Hubble calculated that this spiral nebula lay one million light-years from Earth, or a distance more than three times the most generous estimates of the diameter of the Milky Way itself.

Panek reported:

> In February 1924, Hubble wrote to his former Mount Wilson colleague, Harlow Shapley, then the director of the Harvard College Observatory and a leading proponent of the single-galaxy view of the universe: "You will be interested to hear that I have found a Cepheid variable in the Andromeda Nebula (M31)." Years later, a student of Shapley's recalled the astronomer's receiving this pivotal piece of correspondence, reading it quickly, then holding it out and sighing, "Here is the letter that has destroyed my universe."

Later, on New Year's Day 1925, at the gathering of the American Association for the Advancement of Science in Washington, D.C., a friend presented Hubble's paper with the findings from his research. Hubble himself was absent. This event is a defining moment that divides history neatly in two. Before then, the common conception was that the universe began and ended with our galaxy—period. There were no questions. That was an unequivocal reality. After that date, the universe would consist of however many galaxies astronomers could find.

I think of it this way. We can think of b.h., that is, Before Hubble. We can think of a.h., that is, After Hubble. We now know Hubble underestimated the distance. We now believe Andromeda to be 2.2 million to 2.9 million light-years away. The approximate diameter of the Milky Way has shrunk to only 100,000 light-years. Panek confirms what we have learned since that extraordinary day of January 1, 1925: "From 1925 to 1990, astronomers have discovered 10 billion galaxies. During the decade of 1990 to 2000, thanks to the Hubble Space telescope, the total number of known galaxies has increased exponentially—from 10 billion to 125 billion."

The number is growing as I write and as you read. We live in an ever-expanding universe. We have made a paradigm shift from this planet to the stars.

Joseph and Martha

In the midst of researching and writing this chapter, I remembered a conversation I had with a friend of mine. I will refer to him as Joseph and to his wife as Martha. I want to respect our friendship and their privacy. We have been friends for a long, long time. I have helped as consultant in three of the congregations in which he has served as pastor. Joseph is a good shepherd with his people. He is a helpful preacher. He is a wise, caring leader. He has considerable wisdom and intelligence. He is an excellent pastor with the whole community. He is among the leading pastors in his denomination. We have visited together many times. Joseph and Martha, Julie and I—we are close, good friends and family together. We have grown closer across the years. Joseph and I were sitting on his front porch, enjoying the cool of the evening. During the conversation, he said something of the following to me.

Kennon,

I want to thank you for our friendship over the years. Your wisdom and help in the congregations in which I have served has been more than I can say. These congregations are doing God's mission. They are stronger and healthier for your help. Thank you for your consulting wisdom. Especially, I am most grateful for your friendship with me across the years.

I want you to know how much I am enjoying retirement. I am having fun with Martha, our kids, and our grandchildren. As the saying goes, you have likely heard it before, "If we knew how much fun grandchildren were, we would have had them first." Soon, we will have our fifth grandchild.

I am enjoying the freedom from the pressure of being pastor to so many people. My last church was among the best I have served. They were great people. Martha and I miss them. Yet, I do not now have the burden of being with people in times of illness, death, and funerals. I do not have to deal with troubled marriages, depressed individuals, compulsive personalities, and bossy people. One of the best advantages of retirement is that I do not have to deal with people with whom I prefer not to deal. At the same time, I look back on years of ministry more exceptional than I could ever have imagined when I began.

Now, I am coming to the question with which I would appreciate your help. Your Ph.D. degree is in systematic theology. We have had many long talks together about theology. We have helped one another in deepening our understanding of the Christian life and faith.

You remember that I took up astronomy shortly after retiring. I am amazed at what I have learned about the universe. I am now on my third telescope. Yes, it is the biggest yet. I meet with an astronomy group once a month. We share discoveries and stories. We do night field trips together. One of the fellows has an unusually powerful telescope. With his telescope, we see far into the universe. We find ourselves reading various astronomical journals. We have made a trip to visit one of the largest telescopes on the planet. That was something!

I have a question. I know I am taking a bit to get to it. I would really be grateful for your wisdom.

I believe in the grace of God. I have seen the manifestations of God's grace in so many people and in so many ways across the years. I believe Jesus Christ is our Lord and Savior. I have invited many people to accept Christ in their lives. With gratitude, people tell me I have helped them to discover Christ as the Lord of their lives. I have preached about the birth, life, teachings, death, and the resurrection of Christ. He is central to my preaching and to my whole life.

My question is this, what do I do with Christ and the universe?

Let me put it this way. It was easier for me to believe that Jesus is the one and only Son of God when I thought the universe was smaller than it is. It was easier to believe that Jesus came to save humankind when I believed we were the only people in the universe.

Be at peace. (One of your favorite encouragements; you taught it to me.) I have not gone over to the notion that there is another earth out there. Some suggest there is an exact replica of this earth elsewhere in the universe. I do not think so. Yet, the possibility of life, in some form, grows more probable with each new discovery of the immensity of the universe. I remember, in my history class, learning of that earlier time when humankind thought the earth was flat. I sometimes think that to say there is no other life in the vastness of the universe is a little like continuing to believe that the earth is flat. However, I have not quite settled in my own mind whether there is other life out there. I want to think on this.

Nevertheless, I am puzzled. (Another of your frequent sayings.) Could you help me? In these twilight years of my life, as peaceful as they are, I wonder what we are to do with Christ, the universe, and the mission to which Christ invites us. Several thoughts occur to me.

The first is that we are to take seriously Christ's invitation to go into all of the world. God sent Jesus—once for all time, and only to earth for the entirety of the universe. We are to carry the Good News that Jesus is Lord and Savior to the whole of the universe. We are to take the word, "world," seriously. We are to carry the message of grace throughout the stars. We are to see ourselves, with meekness and humility, as created by God to carry the message of grace to whatever life forms are present in the whole of God's universe. God sent Christ so that we would know the mission God gives to us.

As we do so, we are to avoid the errors of earlier missionaries who superimposed their own culture on the peoples they discovered in the now older "New World." I sometimes think God gave us the "New World" of this earth so that we could learn from our mistakes here before we begin to share God's message of grace elsewhere in the universe. We are to respect whatever cultures we find. We are to honor the best of what earlier missionaries did. With a spirit of grace, we are to share the message of grace throughout the universe. We are to send missionaries into space in the same way the disciples went out in that earliest, first age of mission.

The second thought I have is that Jesus came here first, sent of God. Having come here first, Christ has gone to other places, and will go to other places. In one of our early creeds, we affirm that Jesus "descended into hell." That statement has been thought to confirm what happened to all the peoples who had come before Christ. The creed affirms that Christ saves them as well. We could understand Christ's work in a universal manner—namely, that he goes wherever God sends Him to share (as you would say) the gifts of grace, compassion, community, and hope.

God's love of life is such that God may already have created life somewhere else. If so, it is likely that God has sent His Son there, just as God sent him to earth. If God has not already created life elsewhere, it is likely, because of God's love for life, that God will create life somewhere else. God will send Jesus to share the Word of Grace there. Jesus' way of helping there may be different from how he helped here on earth. We believe his death on the cross was once for all time. We believe his resurrection was once for all time. Thus, his way of helping might be different. God will know best.

The third thought I have is that God's plan is to send His only Son only to earth to share the Gospel of grace only with this earth. God, for whatever reasons, known only to God, does not plan to share the Gospel of grace with other living beings elsewhere in the universe. Under this thought, I have in mind that there may be life forms elsewhere but that God chooses not to send any form of Good News to them. Perhaps, they do not need it, or perhaps God simply chooses to focus God's grace with Earth.

We are not to develop any sense of ego about this. We are not to take an attitude of superiority. Haughtiness and snobbishness are to be avoided. Rather, we are to be humbly grateful that God would share the gift of the Gospel with us. This "exclusive to Earth" thought does not quite match with my sense of the loving grace of God. Yet, I honor the mysteries of God. It may be that God only plans to share His Good News with our Earth.

My fourth thought is that Jesus was sent here—to this earth, and that other messengers of God were sent to other living creatures in other places elsewhere, and may be sent in the future. God sent His only Son to share the Good News with us. Other messengers have gone and/or are going to share God's grace with other life elsewhere in the universe. God makes these decisions.

This thought does not mean that God has several sons, each of whom serves as savior to some life culture somewhere across the universe. I think of Jesus as the only Son of God. It means that God sends messengers that match with whatever life forms exist. These other messengers take on the distinctive life form appropriate to the life beings with whom they are sharing the grace of God.

I think of these four possibilities, and would appreciate your wisdom. I want you to know that I reject three others. First, I reject the notion that Jesus is simply a great man. I do not think this is so. There is more to the mysteries of the Incarnation and Resurrection of Christ than that. Jesus Christ is the Risen Lord.

I am coming slowly to reject a second possibility: that there is no life elsewhere. To say there is no life in the whole of the universe is, I have come to conclude, a little like trying to hold on to the feeble notion that the earth is flat. We have been too egocentric. I am beginning to see that we, meaning humankind, have been egoistic, shortsighted, and wrong so many times. I am almost coming to think that we are as wrong about no life elsewhere as we were that the earth is flat.

What I do know is this: my grandchildren take for granted that there is life elsewhere. They do not give the matter a second thought. As you have often noted, they have never lived in a time when Star Trek was not. I do think about whether there is life elsewhere. Sometimes, I think that God would not create so vast a universe, and with His love for life, not create life elsewhere. I am coming to the sense that God has created and is creating life wherever God wants to do so.

Third, I reject the idea that Jesus is simply an astronaut from another planet. There may be life elsewhere in the universe. Other life forms may have sent their messengers to us. "Astronauts" from other planets may have visited earth. In the future, astronauts may visit our earth. Surprisingly, for myself, I am open to the thought that there may have been and will be other astronauts from other parts of the universe. However, I am confident that Jesus is more than a visiting astronaut. Jesus is the Son of God. Could you share your thoughts with me?

This is not a "pressing" matter. It is one that has come to me in recent times. As I look back on my years of ministry, I am grateful. As I look to the future—whatever that may be, in God's good grace, I live with confidence and hope. I want to thank you for your many kindnesses across the years. I know how busy you are. As you have time, I would be grateful for your wisdom.

∞

We agreed that I would give his question further thought. About this time, Martha invited us in to share one of her wonderful lemon meringue pies.

∞

Universe and Sacrament

I thought about our conversation. I prayed. I cherish our friendship. I thought further. I am grateful for his wisdom. I honor our conversations together across the years. Then, I wrote the following letter to him.

Dear Joseph:

I want to thank you for our visit together. I thought about your question while I was on my recent speaking trip. I was delighted we could share together. It was good to be with you. I have taken a couple of days to rest up from my trip and to think about how best to share my own wisdom in relation to your question. These thoughts come to me. They have to do with immensity and immediacy.

The universe is God's sacramental sign. The immensity of the universe is God's way of teaching us the immensity of God's love with and for us. God wants us to know how immense God's love is for us. God creates the universe as immense as God does so that we will be confident, be assured of the rich, full immensity of God's love for us. The immensity of the universe is God's way of saying, "My love for you is as big as the universe."

Through our recent research, we have learned that the universe is expanding at an accelerating rate. The universe is not only continuing to expand, it is doing so at an increasing rate of expansion. This is God's way of teaching us, that as full and complete as God's love is for us, God's love for us continues to expand at an accelerating rate. God wants us to know how much God loves us.

God teaches us the immediacy of God's love in the manger. God wants us to know how near, how close, how much at hand His love is for us. God sends Jesus—born in a manger— to teach us that God's grace, compassion, and hope are as near as a babe in a manger. Through His birth, teachings, life, death, and resurrection, Christ shares with us the nearness, the closeness, the immediacy of God's love.

God first teaches us the immediacy of His great compassion and hope. And then, as time passes, God helps us to discover the immensity of the universe, and therefore the immensity of God's grace and love in our lives. God, with infinite wisdom, knew that if, at first, He taught us the full immensity of the universe and, thereby, the immensity of His love for us, we human beings might have been "scared off." We might have been so overwhelmed that we could not fully understand the extraordinary immensity of God's love and grace.

Thus, in God's loving kindness and wisdom, God first teaches us the nearness and immediacy of the grace, compassion, and hope with which He blesses our lives. Then, as we more fully begin to appreciate and absorb the rich, full closeness and availability of His grace in our lives, God helps us to discover and comprehend the immensity of the universe and the immensity of God's love for us.

God loves life. I am convinced of this. God has a yearning for life. God is the source of all life. The size of the universe teaches us how immense God's love of life is. Thus, there is a likelihood God has created life elsewhere, or intends to do so at some point in the future. Certainly, the creation of life is not ours to decide. This is God's decision.

I agree with you. Humankind has been too egocentric. I call it egoanthropocentric. We have thought that life comes only in anthropomorphic form. Yes, we are aware of other life forms on our own planet. In recent times, we have come to value these more fully. Moreover, our imaginations have led us to think of other possible life forms elsewhere. Yet, too often, we have been preoccupied with our own selves. Sometimes, we think we are the center of the universe. Fortunately, God's grace stirs us to our deepest humility and our profound gratefulness simply to be alive . . . and loved of God.

I have this confidence. People are drawn to movements that help them make sense of life in this universe as we are now discovering it. People are no longer drawn to institutions that "pretend" that life consists primarily of this planet, this sun, this solar system, and this Milky Way.

Like many, I am open to the possibility that God, with a compelling love for life, may very well have created life elsewhere in the universe or plans to do so at some future time or age. I am amazed at how self-involved we have been as humankind. To believe that there is life nowhere else in the universe comes close to that ancient, false notion that the earth is flat. We cannot limit what God has done or may do. We can be grateful God has given life to us. The irony would be that we would spend half our lives trying to deny life may be elsewhere in the universe, and we are alive, as a gift of God, to do so.

I know this: God's grace is immediate and immeasurable. God, in God's good time, will lead us to a richer, fuller awareness of all of His actions on this planet, in this solar system, in this Milky Way, and beyond.

Of your four suggestions, I am drawn to your first one. I suggest we discuss this further as a promising possibility. My wisdom teaches me that God sent Jesus once, for all life beings, to this Earth. We are invited, of God, to share the Good News of the grace of God throughout the world— meaning, throughout the universe. My mind is less drawn to your second notion—that Jesus came first to Earth, and that he has and/or will go elsewhere in the galaxies. The third suggestion is worth passing by. I am confident God does not intend that the immensity of His grace be limited only to the life forms on this planet. It would be limiting God to suggest that God has no plans to share the Good News elsewhere in the universe. We cannot limit God. God does not limit His grace. At the least, we cannot limit the grace of God.

Your fourth suggestion is an interesting thought on your part—namely, the concept that God sent Jesus to Earth and has sent and/or is sending other messengers to other planets. Certainly, God has sent other messengers to this planet— Abraham, Isaac, Jacob, Moses, the various Prophets, John the Baptist, etc. Our confidence is that Jesus is the full and complete revelation of the grace and love of God. Somehow, to think of other messengers going elsewhere in the universe seems to detract from that understanding.

I grant you that we see the unfolding of God's grace as including other messengers to Earth—for example, Moses, John the Baptist, and so on. Thus, in this same spirit, God may send other messengers to other planets. For now, we are not given to know this. What we know is that we are blessed, generously, abundantly, with the Good News of the grace of God. What we know is that we are invited, with humility and gratefulness, to share this Good News throughout the world.

Our searching of the stars is our searching for God. Our searching of the stars is our searching for new life. Our searching of the stars is our curiosity for new discoveries. Our searching of the stars is our searching to understand ourselves. As humankind, we have searched for New Worlds in the past. Now, we are searching for the New Worlds, given of God, across the universe in the midst of which we live. This searching, this yearning, this longing for discovery is a gift of God.

In recent years, we have experienced a major paradigm shift from this planet to the stars. Some speak of the shift as one from an industrial to a technological culture. Much is made of that shift. Actually, that shift is simply part of the larger shift we have made from Earth to the Universe. In a deeper, larger spirit, the shift to a technological culture is star driven, not the other way around.

We could discuss which came first: the interest in the stars, or the interest in technology. In some ways, such a discussion is a little like discussing which came first, the egg or the chicken. The way I have come to think is this: technology is star driven. Hubble came first; then, technology. Yes, he used the technology of the telescope to discover the stars. The longing to search the stars built the telescope he used.

Our searching drives our technology. Technology is our sailing vessel to the new New World. In olden days, we built wooden sailing ships to search out New Worlds. The ships were the outgrowth of our searching. We did not build the ships, then ask what to do with them. The ships were the vessels for our searching. We do the same today. Now, we build technological ships. Our search for the stars drives our development of new technology. It is not the other way around.

Yes, technology has value and drive, in and for its own advantage. Some people develop technology for the sake of technology, and in relation to its uses on this planet. We often talk of the new uses of technology that have given us advances in education, medicine, research, mathematics, business, etc. We do speak of the technological discoveries in our space programs that have benefit and application on Earth. While all of this it true, there is deeper dynamism to the paradigm shift that has happened.

A primordial driving force in the development of new technology is to search the stars. We search for New Worlds. We are given, of God, a longing, a yearning to search the universe with which God has blessed us. We are amazed at the immensity of the universe. We are amazed at the immediacy of the universe. We learn of God's grace.

Joseph, I am confident that there is a time for the stars, there is a time for this planet, and that *this is the time for the stars.* I am confident that healthy congregations encourage people to make sense of life in the whole of God's universe and on this planet. Healthy congregations do not ignore the discoveries of the universe we are making. They help people make sense of life in the world, in which we discover we now live.

Julie and I look forward to being with you and Martha and having fun together in the near future. Martha makes the best lemon meringue pie I know. We will greatly enjoy sharing one of her pies together. Share our love and best with everyone—especially your children and your grandchildren. The grace of God be with all of you.

Warmly,

Kennon

∞

Since sending my letter to Joseph, I have had further opportunity to reflect on his question. More so, I have reflected on the warmth of our friendship across the years. God gives us the privilege of warm, caring friends with whom we have the honor to live this life. Joseph is such a friend. We have talked since my letter to him. We will talk more. I am deeply grateful for our friendship together.

We live in the stars. We used to live on this planet, looking out, or looking up, at the stars. Our frame of reference was this planet. We now live in the midst of the stars. I am grateful Joseph and I, and you, live in the stars together.

4

The Cultural Shift to Excellent Sprinters

Therefore, since we are surrounded by so great a cloud of witnesses, let us also lay aside every weight, and sin which clings so closely, and let us run with perseverance the race that is set before us. . . .

—Hebrews 12:1

There is a time for excellent sprinters. There is a time for solid marathon runners. This is a time for excellent sprinters. We now live in an excellent sprinter culture.

We used to live in a solid marathon runner culture. In that earlier time, both the culture and congregations focused on this pattern of behavior. The theology of the Christian life concentrated on people living as solid marathon runners. The culture reinforced this. In our time, excellent sprinter behavior is more effective than solid marathon runner behavior. Solid marathon runner behavior is effective. Excellent sprinter behavior is more effective.

We have seen a major paradigm shift from a solid marathon culture to an excellent sprinter culture. Thus one possibility for reaching and growing the grass roots is to help people develop a balance of excellent sprinter and solid marathon runner behavior patterns. A healthy, effective congregation, in this new time, helps people learn this balance. These congregations share this balance in their life together and in their mission in the world.

About half the people I have known in life are solid marathon runners. About half the people I have known in life are excellent sprinters. Solid marathon runners do what they do routinely, regularly, weekly, monthly, year in year out. Excellent sprinters do what they do in short-term, highly intensive ways, near the time at hand.

Solid marathon runners pack for vacation three weeks ahead and by departure date have checked what they packed four times. Excellent sprinters are packing for vacation as the car is leaving the drive. Both have fun on the same vacation. Solid marathon runners play a golf course by playing the front nine and then conclude by playing the back nine. Excellent sprinters play the course one hole at a time, one stroke at a time. They both have fun playing the same course.

Solid marathon runners work on their quilting project regularly, systematically, steadily, block by block, day by day. Excellent sprinters work on their project in a series of short-term, highly intensive sprints, including a fall and spring quilting retreat. Both create beautiful quilts. Solid marathon runners study two hours every night. Excellent sprinters study the two nights before the exam. Both do well when they take the exam.

At many dinner tables, solid marathon runner parents and their excellent sprinter children have tense, difficult discussions over homework. The solid marathon runner parents insist that their children study two hours every night. Excellent sprinter children can sit for two hours with the book, turn the pages, and at the end of the time not know what they have almost read.

With excellent sprinter children, the art is to help them learn the way they learn, not the way their parents learn. The art is to turn homework into a short-term, highly intensive project: Monday is math; Tuesday is English; Wednesday is spelling; Thursday is history; and so on. The projects, for each night, may vary from one week to the next. The key is to turn homework into a distinct excellent sprinter project, and to complete each project within a specific, short period of time.

Solid marathon pastors do their preaching preparation three hours each day, Monday through Friday, and success-fully prepare a helpful sermon. Excellent sprinters do their sermon preparation on Friday, or Friday night, or Saturday, or Saturday night, or at 5:00 on Sunday morning.

Actually, excellent sprinters do two forms of sermon preparation. They prepare the sermon in the short, highly intensive time just before Sunday. They also do what I call "four-for-three." They take four days for the coming three months. They discover a quiet place in their community or go away on a peaceful retreat. In this short, intensive time away, they study, think, pray, and relax. They look at the coming three months. They discover where they are headed for the four major-major sermons during the coming three months.

They look first for the four major-major Sundays rather then sequentially at all thirteen weeks ahead. During October, November, and December, Christmas would be a major-major Sunday. Easter, in February, March, April, would be one. They also develop some hint of four other sermons. Palm Sunday would be one. Now, it is a Friday during the second month before a major-major Sunday. They are not starting from scratch. They hit the ground running because that particular sermon has been mulling around in their mind since their excellent sprinter sermon preparation time nearly two months before. (In *Preaching Grace,* I discuss sermon preparation more fully, and I commend the book to you.)

In coaching my basketball teams, I knew I was working with youths who live life as excellent sprinters. On Monday, we worked on our fast break. Tuesday, we worked on our full-court press. Wednesday, we worked on man-to-man defense. Thursday was foul shooting. On Friday, we worked on our offensive plays. In a way, we never practiced every night of the week. What we did do was to work on this project and then another project over the week.

In coaching the drama groups I have had the privilege of directing, we followed a similar spirit. We would work on Monday on the first part of Act I. Tuesday, the focus might be the middle of Act III. On Wednesday the focus might be Act II. Thursday, the focus might be the concluding part of Act III. Friday, the focus might be the latter part of Act I. We would start with the simplest parts of the drama, then work our way to the more difficult parts. We turned our "weekly rehearsals" into five short-term, highly intensive, excellent sprints. The kids in the drama groups, most of whom were excellent sprinters, thrived. They did not think of themselves as coming to a rehearsal every night. They thought of our preparation as working on this project and then on another project.

Solid marathon runners come to worship *every* Sunday. Excellent sprinters come to worship *each* Sunday. Both of them are there forty to fifty Sundays a year. The emphasis on "be sure to be in church every Sunday" appeals to the solid marathon runner. The emphasis on "look forward to worship this coming Sunday" appeals to the excellent sprinter.

Being a solid marathon runner and an excellent sprinter are distinctive ways of thinking, planning, behaving, feeling, acting, and living. How we think is how we behave. It is more than semantics or a play on words. People think, behave, act, plan, and live in these distinctive ways.

I was having this discussion in a congregation where one of the key leaders runs and wins national marathons. He said to me with considerable delight, "Dr. Callahan, I've discovered that I'm an excellent sprinter. Years ago, when I began training, running, and winning, the way I planned and thought of the race was to run 'mile one' in a certain amount of time. Then, I would run the *new* mile one, not a second mile, but a new mile one, in a certain amount of time. What I've been doing over the years is running twenty-six excellent sprints back-to-back."

Grandchildren are God's gift to help those of us who have learned how to be a solid marathon runner learn how to be an excellent sprinter. Grandchildren are excellent sprinters. When we behave with them as solid marathon runner grandparents, they tend to visit less frequently. What mostly happens is this: grandparents discover the considerable delight, pleasure, and satisfaction they experience being with their grandchildren. It is amazing how quickly grandparents learn to think, plan, behave, act, and live as excellent sprinters. They have fun sharing in short-term, highly intensive projects with their grandchildren.

People visit with me about the difficulties their children are having in school. We talk at great length. It is true that some children wrestle with attention deficit disorder. It is equally true that sometimes the difficulty has to do with the fact that a solid marathon runner teacher is teaching excellent sprinter kids. The marathon teacher is persistently insisting that the kids learn the way the teacher, as a marathoner, learns. The kids are trying to teach the marathon teacher that they do not learn that way. Most kids do not have a lack of attention; they have considerable attention—for short-term, highly intensive projects.

I have lost track of the number of conversations Sunday school teachers have had with me about discipline problems with children in their classes. I listen and learn. Mostly, what I discover is that it is not a discipline problem. What exists is a solid marathon runner Sunday school teacher trying to teach excellent sprinter kids in solid marathon runner ways. The excellent sprinter kids are trying to teach their teacher that they do not learn the way the teacher teaches.

Likewise, I have lost count of the number of conversations couples have had with me. They have discovered, with considerable delight, that one of them has the gifts of a solid marathon runner and one has the gifts of an excellent sprinter. They share with me how they have learned to appreciate, value, and benefit from the complementary competencies they bring to their marriage. They share with me that they now have a better understanding of some of their difficulties. The solid marathon runner expected solid marathon runner behavior from his or her spouse, who is an excellent sprinter. The reverse also happened. The art is to discover the advantages these complementary competencies bring to the marriage.

These are learned patterns of behavior. No one is genetically born either a solid marathon runner or an excellent sprinter. We can learn both patterns of behavior. Having learned both ways of thinking and behaving, we can decide that, in a given situation, the valuable behavior pattern is to behave like an excellent sprinter, while in another situation the valuable behavior pattern is to behave like a solid marathon runner. We can grow both. No one is locked into one or the other behavior pattern. You can learn both and benefit from the advantages of both.

The Cultural Shift

In *Future Shock*, Alvin Toffler talks about three major shifts that have happened in the course of human history. These are the shift from nomad to agrarian, from agrarian to industrial, and, in recent times, from industrial to technological. As you have seen in Chapter Three, I view this third shift more fully as the shift from our planet to the stars.

Further, I advance Toffler's work in this way: the nomad culture was a solid marathon runner culture. It followed the seasons, the herds, and the water regularly and routinely, season after season, year after year. With the exception of two welcomed sprints (planting and harvest), the agrarians were also solid marathon runners. Their lives were mostly regular and routine, day in day out, week in week out, month after month. The industrial period continued the solid marathon runner culture. There may have been a peak season near Christmas, but mostly it was producing X number of products per hour, per day, per week, per month, year in year out.

Major Cultural Shifts

Nomad	Solid marathon runner
Agrarian	Solid marathon runner
Industrial	Solid marathon runner
Technological	Excellent sprinter

In our time, we have experienced the paradigm shift to a stars (technological) culture and concomitantly the shift to an excellent sprinter culture. In prior times, the culture reinforced, rewarded, and encouraged the behavior patterns of the solid marathon runner. In our time, the culture encourages, reinforces, and rewards the behavior patterns of the excellent sprinter.

Remember the parable of the hare and the tortoise? Who won? The tortoise. Why? The parable was written by a solid marathon runner culture, and the point of the parable was to support the idea that if you wanted to succeed in life, you would be and behave like the solid marathon runner tortoise, not like the excellent sprinter hare. In our time, the hare wins. The tortoise finishes the race. The hare wins.

That is my way of confirming that in our time, the culture reinforces, encourages, and rewards excellent sprinter behavior patterns. Sometimes, a person asks if there is a possibility for the middle-distance runner. The answer is yes. I go on to point out that the purpose of the parable, written by a solid marathon culture, was to reinforce marathon behavior. There is no middle-distance runner in the parable. The purpose was not to allow for various individual learnings and behaviors. The intent of the culture and the parable was to suggest that one would be successful in life by behaving like a solid marathon runner.

Another way to think of it is this. In a solid marathon runner culture, six or seven out of ten people might behave as solid marathon runners, and the culture would confirm their behavior. The other three or four excellent sprinters would see themselves as out of place. They would be taught by the culture that they are misfits. In our time, indeed in the last twenty-five years, this major cultural shift means that six or seven out of ten are excellent sprinters in behavior. The culture rewards and reinforces their behavior. The three or four solid marathon runners now feel like misfits.

The cultural shift to an excellent sprinter culture has grave implications for the Christian movement. A few years ago, a group gathered several of us as major resource persons to address the question "Where is the Christian movement headed in the twenty-first century?" One in our group shared thoughtful wisdom and suggested the decline in religion was really the decline in social conformity and the increase in freedom of choice. I found this a helpful suggestion.

I advance the suggestion in two ways. First, it is more appropriate to discuss the decline in church rather than the decline in religion. There is no decline in religion. My research and that of others indicate that the interest in religion is surging and soaring. The relevant point is that the current interest in religion is not connecting with the institutional church. It is therefore more helpful to confirm the decline in church interest, not the decline in religion.

Second, there are several reasons for the decline in church interest. The decline in social conformity and the increase in freedom of choice are major contributing factors to the decline in church. I would add that the increase in new forms of social conformity that do not include church is an equally major contributing factor. Social conformity has not left us. It is still with us. It no longer includes church.

Moreover and most significant, among the reasons for the decline in church interest is the lingering of customs, habits, and traditions of a churched culture that matched the solid marathon culture of that earlier time. Those customs, habits, and traditions worked well for that culture; it was a solid marathon runner culture. They do not work well in our time.

Now, we have people who come with a search for community, not for a culture of committees. We have people who come looking for excellent sprinter possibilities for mission, shepherding, worshipping, study, recreation, and fellowship. What they frequently encounter, however, is a pattern of solid marathon runner behavior. One of the lingering customs, habits, and traditions that are most disastrous for churches in our time is the focus, solely or primarily, on solid marathon runner patterns of behavior in a congregation.

A healthy congregation behaves as a movement, lives compassion, helps people develop a theology of the stars, and encourages excellent sprinters. This congregation is strong and constructive. It has a promising future. A congregation that behaves as an institution, stresses commitment, focuses on a limited appreciation of the universe, and rewards only solid marathon runner behavior is weak and declining. This congregation has a future of retrenching, retreating, and dying.

How People Grow

Both people and congregations grow whole, healthy lives in five ways:

- One time
- Seasonally
- In the short term, in three to five sessions
- In the long term, six or more sessions
- Weekly, monthly, year-round

Many people grow in one-time ways. AA and Al-Anon are major movements in which people discover how to live whole, healthy lives in one-time ways. No one gives up drinking for life, or gives it up weekly, monthly, year-round. They give it up one day at a time, in one-time ways. Countless millions of people benefit from this one-time way of growing a whole, healthy life.

The Emmaus Walk, Promise Keepers, revivals, and intensive personal growth seminars are all ways in which people grow their lives forward in a one-time event. Young Life has built much of its mission with youth on "come, one time, to a camp in Colorado and discover the grace of God in your life." Many, many camps and retreats are one-time events that decisively change people's lives. In my interviews with people, they share with me, again and again, the one-time events that have advanced and shaped their lives.

Habitat for Humanity is a one-time approach to mission. People are invited to come and build one house. I know people who have helped build one house every year for eight years, but they never "signed up to build a house every year." What they did was to sign up to build one house. They had so much fun and gained so much satisfaction that they decided to sign up to build one house again. Looking back, they are surprised to see that they actually helped build eight houses.

Many healthy congregations offer one-time mission projects, one-time Bible studies, one-time fellowship events, and one-time activities for children and youth. These one-time events help people grow whole, healthy lives.

In one of the churches I have helped over the years, the pastor and I talked about how to help with the deep grief existing in their congregation following the deaths of several children that year. It was important to offer comfort and compassion. I suggested he offer, in November of that year, a one-time seminar on grieving. I suggested November because this would be near the first Christmas without the life and joy of the children who had died.

The seminar was held on a Saturday morning with three sessions: 8:30 to 10:00, 10:30 to noon, and the third session over a wonderful lunch together. During the course of the morning, he led the people gathered through the stages of grief. They shared in learning, singing, praying, and mutual conversation. It was a great help. They came to terms with their loss. People were at peace.

As the event was coming to an end, the pastor asked, "Has this been helpful?" "Oh, yes, pastor," he heard. "This has been extraordinarily helpful." Then, being a solid marathon runner, he went on to say, "Well, maybe we should meet every month." Their reply was, "Oh no, pastor. You've helped us. We're at peace. What we'll be glad to do is to sponsor the seminar next year for those who may lose a loved one this coming year." What they were doing was turning a one-time event into a seasonal event.

We share in many seasonal events in which we grow and develop as whole, healthy persons. Vacation Bible school is a seasonal event that, in a one-week, short-term, highly intensive way, helps children discover the Christian life richly and fully. Healthy congregations offer many seasonal mission projects, Bible studies, recreational events, and fellowship gatherings.

I was in an airport and struck up a conversation with a group of couples who were laughing, carrying on, and having a good time together. We were waiting to board the same plane. We visited. They were flying to meet some other friends. They had all graduated from the same college. Their group gathered once a year to share a sense of community, roots, place, and belonging, of being together as a sharing, caring family. They have been gathering for more than thirty years. There are notes, telephone calls, e-mails, and personal visits during the year. At the same time, this seasonal grouping is seeing them through much of this life's pilgrimage.

Julie participates in a quilting retreat in the fall and a quilting retreat in the spring. Quilting seminars are held during each retreat. Working early in the morning and late into the night, many quilt projects are completed. Moreover, much more happens at a quilting retreat than just quilting. Lasting friendships are built that lead to frequent conversations, notes, get-togethers, and e-mails across the entire year. This seasonal grouping shares family with one another.

Short-term ways of growing are best done in three to five sessions, over three to five weeks, or three to five months. Any time you are tempted to offer something six sessions long—whether it is a mission project, a study group, a recreational opportunity, or a series of fellowship possibilities—

I encourage you to do three to five sessions. You will reach both excellent sprinters and solid marathon runners.

When we announce something that is more than five sessions long, we have announced, in effect, that this is "for solid marathon runners only." Excellent sprinters will do three, four, or five sessions. You see this in participation level. A group gathers. There is excellent attendance the first time. The second time, the attendance is still good, but by the sixth time the attendance has fallen off considerably. The excellent sprinters have participated as much as they plan to for now and have moved on to other projects.

In a congregation in which I have worked over the years, the pastor is an excellent Bible teacher. One year, he offered a nine-session Bible study on the life of Christ. He had an excellent response. I suggested he offer three sessions on the birth of Christ and the beginning of Christ's teachings. This could be during the season of Advent as we headed to Christmas. He could offer three sessions during Lent as Easter approached. He could offer the final three sessions as we approached Pentecost. He did. The participation in his Bible study increased more than 400 percent. Did the excellent sprinters attend all nine sessions? No; they participated in three sessions, then in three sessions, and then in three sessions.

Recently, I was helping a wonderful congregation as a consultant. They are healthy and thriving. Their part-time choir director and I were visiting together. He is a most gifted musician. In that state, he is considered the finest high school choral director in all of the public schools. In the summer, youths come from all over the nation to his choral clinics.

He said, "Dr. Callahan, we're having this difficulty in our children's choirs. Many of our children drop out of choir in third and fourth grade and instead join soccer teams. This happens even with some of the children who love music the most. Can you help us?"

I said to him, "On the soccer team, the pattern is: we practice on Wednesday; we play on Saturday. One practice. One game. In your children's choirs the pattern is: we practice, we practice, we practice, we practice, we practice, we practice, we practice, we practice; then, we sing. You do not do this with your adult choir. They practice on Wednesday, then sing on Sunday. Think of what the drop-out rate among adults would be, if there were eight or more practices before they could sing."

He made the connection with his own high school choir. As good as he is, and as good as his choir is, he has a retention problem with some of his best singers. His pattern has been that they rehearse all semester long, then give one performance. In some years, they have rehearsed both fall and spring semesters, then given one concert for the whole school year. He concluded that his high school choir needed to sing more frequently. He clearly saw that the children's choirs in his church needed to do so.

My Ph.D. is in systematic theology. Ph.D. degrees are designed by solid marathon runners to be achieved by solid marathon runners. I have had the privilege of teaching for many years in a distinguished seminary. A high density of Ph.D. professors teach in seminaries. Who invented semesters? Solid marathon runners. Thus, seminaries operate by semesters and are designed by and for solid marathon runners.

You can actually learn the same amount of material in a short-term, highly intensive three-week summer course, or an interterm intensive course between the fall and spring semesters. People do it all the time. Several universities in our country are moving toward a curriculum in which the students take one course for five weeks; then they take another course for five weeks. It is a short-term, highly intensive, successful approach to learning. Excellent sprinters thrive.

Long-term possibilities are six or more sessions long. Many people grow as they include themselves in Bible study groupings, mission projects, recreational events, and fellowship gatherings that are long-term. These long-term possibilities appeal primarily to solid marathon runners. The same is true for weekly, monthly, and year-round possibilities for growing. Solid marathon runners are drawn to these possibilities.

In many congregations, it is the committees within the congregation who plan the mission, shepherding, worship, Bible study, recreational, fellowship, and other kinds of possibilities. It is not accidental, then, that many of these are scheduled to meet on a long-term basis—weekly, monthly, year-round. Committees schedule them. There is a high density of solid marathon runners on committees. It takes being a solid marathon runner to endure all the committee meetings. Thus the opportunities offered, year after year, to the whole congregation are primarily solid marathon runner possibilities, that is, long-term and weekly, or monthly year-round scheduled activities.

When a congregation is wise enough to offer a high density of one-time, seasonal, and short-term possibilities, these benefits result:

• You develop more leaders. For example, you decide to have eight one-time events during the year. A leader comes forward for each one-time event. Eight leaders are grown. Many people will lead a one-time event. However, if a committee lumps eight one-time events into a series of eight, what happens is that we are lucky to get one leader who will do the series of eight.

• With one-time, seasonal, and short-term events, you grow more volunteers. People are glad to volunteer for a one-time event, a seasonal possibility, or a short-term activity. This matches how they live life.

- You have more participants. It is amazing. Both excellent sprinters and solid marathon runners have fun participating in one-time, seasonal, and short-term opportunities for their growth and development.
- You have more excellent results. Many people advance and develop, grow and build their lives through one-time, seasonal, and short-term events.
- You can advance new ways. Would you like to initiate some change within the congregation? The best way to accomplish this is through a one-time event. A one-time change is simply that: a one-time change. People discover in a one-time event that it works well. There is no effort to immediately turn it into a long-term permanent change. We might do it again for just one time. Possibly a third time, for just one time. This helps us discover whether this change matches us well and advances God's mission. We discover whether this change helps people grow and develop whole, healthy lives.
- We learn from excellent mistakes. Another benefit is that out of eight one-time events we do, six work well, and two may be excellent mistakes. The key is that they are one-time excellent mistakes. For example, the way to start a new grouping is to have a one-time event. Have another one-time event; have another one-time event. Let the group discover one another in several one-time gatherings. Then let them decide the rhythm and pace for gathering that works for them. They may decide to be a seasonal group, or a short-term group in the fall, or a short-term group in the spring. Regrettably, what solid marathon runners do when they want to start a new group is to announce that it will meet weekly, beginning three weeks hence. Just enough people who are dysfunctional with one another show up. Now what? We now feel compelled to keep this group propped up, even though it is a group that probably never should have been. When you do one-time possibilities, you keep open the door

allowing you to make one-time excellent mistakes, learn from them, and move on.

Countless congregations are strong and healthy precisely because they reap these benefits from one-time, seasonal, and short-term possibilities.

Many pastors and congregations visit with me about their life together. Mostly, I find excellent matches. Richard is an excellent sprinter. His congregation is an excellent sprinter congregation. It is an excellent match. Sue is a solid marathon runner. Her congregation comprises primarily solid marathon runners. It is an excellent match.

Richard and his congregation sponsor many one-time opportunities for growth and development. They offer numerous seasonal and short-term possibilities. This resonates well with the whole congregation, which consists primarily of excellent sprinters. Sue offers a variety of long-term as well as weekly, monthly, year-round possibilities. This resonates well with her congregation, most of whom grow whole, healthy lives forward in long-term and weekly, monthly, year-round ways.

Sometimes, regrettably, I discover excellent mismatches. Bob is an excellent sprinter. His congregation is a solid marathon runner congregation. Bob focuses on many one-time, seasonal, and short-term opportunities for growth and development. His congregation yearns for long-term and weekly, monthly, year-round opportunities. The match does not work well. They have an excellent mismatch.

Mary is a solid marathon runner. Her congregation is an excellent sprinter congregation. It is an excellent mismatch. Mary is eager to do many long-term and weekly, monthly, year-round activities. However, her congregation is drawn to one-time, seasonal, and short-term possibilities for growth and development. The match does not work well.

Moreover, in our time, the highest density of community people who are unchurched are mostly excellent sprinters. Thus, Richard's congregation thrives in reaching unchurched, excellent sprinter people. Mary's congregation does reasonably well in reaching unchurched people in the community. This is because the excellent sprinters in her congregation reach unchurched excellent sprinters through relational and vocational networks in the community. The congregation sort of puts up with Mary's solid marathon behavior.

The congregations that Sue and Bob serve do not do well in reaching unchurched people in the community. Sue's congregation has two counts against it. One, she is a solid marathon runner. Two, her congregation is a solid marathon congregation. The message out front is, "No room in the inn for excellent sprinters." Bob is an excellent sprinter and has some gifts in reaching unchurched people in the community who are excellent sprinters. However, when they encounter his solid marathon congregation, they shortly discover they do not belong.

Another way to puzzle through how people grow is to look at how people give. The art is to grow generous givers. In our time, we grow generous givers by making available both excellent sprinter and solid marathon runner possibilities of giving. I discuss this material at some length in my book *Giving and Stewardship*, wherein you will discover a discussion on the six sources of giving. For our purposes now, let us look at some examples.

Congregation A is a small, strong congregation that encourages both excellent sprinter and solid marathon runner giving.

Spontaneous	$30,000
Major community Sundays	8,000
Special planned offerings	7,000

Major project	110,000
Annual	100,000
Enduring	40,000
Total giving	$295,000

By contrast, Congregation B, with similar strengths and size, focuses only on solid marathon giving.

Spontaneous	Not encouraged
Major community Sundays	Not encouraged
Special planned offerings	Not encouraged
Major project	Not encouraged
Annual	$100,000
Enduring	Not encouraged
Total giving	$100,000

The only source of giving that is available is making a pledge to the annual budget. The five excellent sprinter sources of giving are not available. The consequence is that people who give in excellent sprinter ways share their generosity with groupings such as the Salvation Army and others that encourage excellent sprinter giving.

Congregation C is a large, regional one that encourages both excellent sprinter and solid marathon runner giving.

Spontaneous	$150,000
Major community Sundays	40,000
Special planned offerings	60,000
Major project	600,000
Annual	500,000
Enduring	200,000
Total giving	$1,550,000

By contrast, Congregation D, again with comparable strengths and size, concentrates only on solid marathon runner giving and openly discourages excellent sprinter giving.

Spontaneous	Not encouraged
Major community Sundays	Not encouraged
Special planned offerings	Not encouraged
Major project	Not encouraged
Annual	$500,000
Enduring	Not encouraged
Total giving	$500,000

The mantra of congregations B and D is that "we will ask you to make only one pledge: to give weekly to the annual budget." In both congregations, there is a high density of marathon runners on the finance committees. Their message is, "If you were really committed, you would give the way we give and the way we want you to give, rather than the way you are inclined to give." They close all the "giving doors" that are excellent sprinter in nature. They focus only on the one source of giving that fits solid marathon runners.

Congregations A and C open all six giving doors. They are aware that pledging to the annual budget is a solid marathon runner way of giving. They know that excellent sprinters, as well as solid marathon runners, give generously in spontaneous, major community Sunday, special planned offering, major project giving, and enduring gift ways. They encourage these five of the six sources of giving and create generous givers.

People grow and give in one-time; seasonal; short-term; long-time; and weekly, monthly, year-round ways. In our early years, we developed our capacity to grow in one of these ways more than in the others. We may have learned a propensity or inclination toward one or two. We can learn to advance and build whole, healthy lives, benefiting from and drawing on all of these ways. All are available to you. God gives you the gift of all five possibilities for growing and developing.

Learn What Works for You

The art of developing a healthy life and an effective congregation are the same: share all five ways of growing with the whole congregation. Learn what works for you. Learn what works for other people. They may or may not be the same. People can develop with all five possibilities. At a given point in their life's pilgrimage, people have developed some of these five more than others.

In our time, we are drawn to congregations that help us grow in ways that match how we grow. We are not drawn to groups who insist, however quietly and politely, that we should grow the way they grow, or that we should grow the way someone else thinks we should grow. Too many solid marathon runners insist that the primary way to grow is the way solid marathon runners grow. Their message is, "You should grow yourself the way I grow myself." Indeed, they go on to suggest that "You should not grow yourself the way you want to grow yourself."

It is the old question: "Must one become a Jew before one can become a Christian? Must one become a solid marathon runner before one can become a Christian?" Or, to turn the question the other way, "Can an excellent sprinter become a Christian?"

Solid marathon runners frequently say to me, "Dr. Callahan, excellent sprinters lack commitment." They have in mind that excellent sprinters do not demonstrate their commitment in long-term and weekly, monthly, year-round ways. It is interesting to consider the Olympics. Long ago, the Olympics started with the marathon run. In our time, what people watch are the excellent sprints. I have yet to meet a single person who says to me that they sat on the edge of their chair watching every single step of the cross-country runs. What people watch is the last four minutes when the cross-country runners come into the stadium and do their last laps.

Excellent sprinters at the Olympics are deeply committed. With total intensity of mind and muscle, they rise from the blocks at the starter's gun and invest—with extraordinary commitment—their whole being in that excellent sprint to the finish line. They will turn around and do another excellent sprint, and another, and another. They share their commitment in short-term, highly intensive, excellent sprinter ways. They do not share their commitment in cross-country marathon runner ways.

In the New Testament, John is the solid marathon runner, and Peter is the excellent sprinter. When the soldiers arrive in the Garden of Gethsemane, Peter responds in a short-term, highly intensive manner. In the closing of the Gospel of John, we discover another example of Peter sprinting. The disciples have been out fishing all night. They are tired and weary, forlorn and desolate. Their boat is empty. The cause with Jesus is gone. Sunrise dawning, they head to shore. A stranger, standing on the beach, calls out to them, "Have you caught any fish?" There is a plaintive, woeful plea in their answer, "No, we haven't caught any fish." "Cast your nets on the right side of the boat," says the stranger. They do. The nets are now so loaded with fish that they cannot bring them into the boat. It dawns on them. The stranger is really Christ. What does Peter do? He leaps from the boat and sprints to shore to embrace his Lord. God blesses both excellent sprinters and solid marathon runners.

An effective, healthy congregation encourages all five ways people advance and develop their lives. You can look at the church bulletin board and the newsletter and discover a healthy balance of possibilities for growth. The healthy balance of possibilities they offer is essentially 8–6–4–2–1. They offer approximately eight one-time possibilities, six seasonal possibilities, four short-term possibilities, two long-term possibilities, and one weekly or monthly possibility.

They know that a high density of people in their congregation, and in the population of unchurched people around them in the community, are excellent sprinters. They have a sense of balance and proportion about what they offer. They understand that both excellent sprinters and solid marathon runners are drawn to one-time, seasonal, and short-term opportunities for growth and development in the Christian life. They are aware that only solid marathon runners are drawn to long-term and weekly, monthly, year-round possibilities.

Offered Possibilities for Growth in a Strong, Healthy Congregation

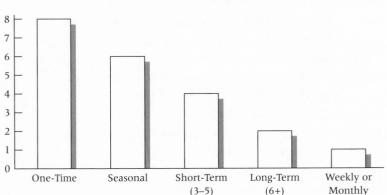

Healthy congregations offer many seasonal and short-term Bible studies. They are wise enough to know that solid marathon Bible study programs work well for people who have learned to be solid marathon runners. They know those Bible studies were written by solid marathon runners. They may offer some marathon Bible studies. As healthy congregations, they have the wisdom to value one-time, seasonal, and short-term possibilities for mission, Bible study, shepherding, groupings, recreation, and fellowship.

These strong congregations share major community Sundays as central to their services of worship. I encourage you to see my book *Dynamic Worship* for a fuller discussion of these Sundays. For now, it is helpful to know that healthy congregations include one-time major community Sundays as part of worship. These major Sundays include Easter and Christmas, plus usually eight more over the course of the year. Worship is gathered around these major community Sundays, and around the short-term, excellent sprinter seasons of the church year.

Worship is thought of, planned, prayed for, and lived out in these one-time and short-term services and seasons. Solid marathon runners think of worship as happening regularly, weekly, fifty-two Sundays of the year, week after week. Excellent sprinters see worship as happening in the services and seasons that draw us close to the grace of God. A healthy congregation does these services extraordinarily well; in effect, it shares these one-time worship services and seasons inside a weekly worship service.

The art that a strong, healthy congregation has discovered is to make available mission, shepherding, worship, study, recreation, and fellowship possibilities in all five ways in which people grow. People resonate with this balance of possibilities. They discover they can grow and develop a whole, healthy life in whatever ways work for them.

Offered Possibilities for Growth in a Weak, Declining Congregation

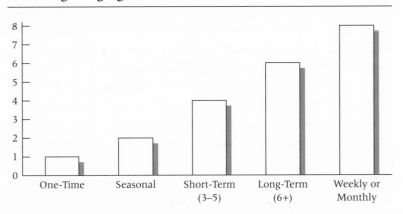

Some congregations are weak and declining. They do not make available all five of these possibilities. They focus on, they emphasize, two ways that people grow, namely, long-term or else weekly, monthly, year-round.

They may offer a few one-time, seasonal, and short-term events as teasers. They see these as the come-on events to attract people to the congregation. However, these are almost incidental. Their real message is that "if you are really going to be a Christian, then you will think, behave, act, and live your life as we do, as solid marathon runners." Their way of behaving as solid marathon runners worked well for them, when it was a solid marathon culture.

They remember the long-term and weekly, monthly, year-round activities in which many people participated. They look at the pictures of those gatherings forty, fifty, and sixty years ago and wonder why there are fewer people in that type of gathering today than there were back then. They have cause to wonder. The fields are white unto the harvest. It is an extraordinary mission field in our time.

Although they are willing to offer one-time, seasonal, and short-term events to hook people in, once the person has gotten somewhat involved in the congregation, they do a bait-and-switch. That is, they say to the person, "Well, we did those one-time, short-term, and seasonal events to get you here. Now that you are here, we want you to switch to the long-term and weekly, monthly, year-round ways. We prefer them. They are the ones we primarily offer. That is the way we primarily want you to live. That is the way we like to live." It is not accidental that these congregations are weak and declining.

Some congregations have decided to die. They have no good reason to do so. Most congregations have more people around them today than ever before. Even so, in our present culture, it is no longer the thing to do to go to church; thus a congregation no longer needs to worry about stealing members from other churches because there are not that many church members to steal. Further, there are so many un-churched people in our communities that it is amazing.

What happens in such a congregation is that the members make an unconscious decision to die. Oh, they do not gather and formally vote on that decision. What they do, informally, is decide to offer only long-term or weekly, monthly, year-round options. They offer virtually no one-time, seasonal, or short-term events, even as teasers. Their message is, "We are solid marathon runners. We think that is the only way one can live as a Christian. We do not think much of excellent sprinters. If you want to join us, you will need to think, act, behave, and live as we do—as marathon runners. This is what we offer."

They offer limited options. When people do not respond to their invitation, they lay the lack of response on the belief that "people are too busy now to go to church." The truth is that people were equally busy in the solid marathon culture

Offered Possibilities for Growth in a Dying Congregation

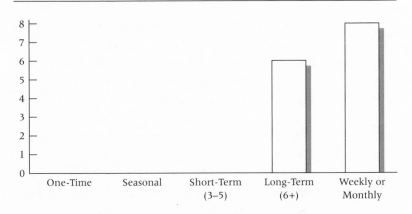

of an earlier time. They were running five solid marathon runs simultaneously, and they were very busy. What happens in our time is that people are now running five excellent sprints simultaneously, but they are no busier now than they were back then.

The significant factor today is that the pace has changed. We were busy with five marathon runs back then; we are now busy with five excellent sprints. Further, we are looking for a grouping that can help us learn how to sprint in a healthy, wholesome, constructive way. We are not looking for the grouping that tells us that our excellent sprinter way of life is wrong. We have the sense, intuition, and feeling to know that the current culture is an excellent sprinter culture, and for us to survive and thrive our ability to deliver excellent sprinter behavior is decisive.

Indeed, I think that without being taught or told, children learn, almost intuitively, by osmosis, that we live in an excellent sprinter culture. They develop the behavior patterns that they sense allow them to survive and thrive in the excellent sprinter culture.

What is true for congregations is true for people. Some people choose to live a strong, healthy life in the grace of God. In their living, they draw on all five possibilities for growing and developing a strong, healthy life. They have available to them one-time, seasonal, short-term, long-term, and weekly or monthly ways of growing and developing. They exercise all five from time to time appropriately to advance their growth.

Some people have chosen to live a weak and declining life. They decide that they want to live a sort of midrange level of life. Christ comes and offers us abundant, full life. They decide not to live life in that spirit. They focus on long-term and weekly or monthly possibilities for living life. They may occasionally participate in a one-time, seasonal, or short-term possibility, but mostly they see these experiences as less helpful. They do not include all five possibilities available for their growth. They limit themselves to two, with an occasional dipping in to the other three. To them, life is sort of, almost, now and then satisfying and fulfilling.

Some people, like some congregations, decide to live a dying life. For them, life is one sad event, one bad event after another. Life is a series of lamentings, complainings, bemoanings, and whinings. They feel out of place in our current times. God gives them all five possibilities. They limit themselves to only two of the five ways people develop. They have a quiet disdain for the other possibilities. They think poorly of people who grow in these other ways. They limit themselves; they limit life to only long-term and weekly or monthly ways of living.

On occasion, excellent sprinters limit themselves to one-time and seasonal possibilities, but I find the vast majority of excellent sprinters are open to all five possibilities. Frequently, in fact, they live out weekly, monthly, year-round behavior much like the solid marathon runner who runs twenty-six one-time excellent sprints. Mostly, excellent sprinters have a spirit of openness to all five possibilities.

Sometimes, solid marathon runners compare the best of being a marathon runner with the worst of being an excellent sprinter. They seek to convince themselves of their own self-righteousness and the rightness of their own way of living. On occasion, excellent sprinters do the same. They compare the best of being an excellent sprinter with the worst of being a solid marathon runner. They seek to convince themselves of their own self-righteousness and the rightness of their way of living. Both of these are a best-to-worst comparison.

The truth is that many solid marathon runners live a whole, healthy life, with a spirit of discipline and discipleship. Some do not. Likewise, many excellent sprinters live a whole, healthy life, with a spirit of discipline and discipleship. Some do not. The art is to do a best-to-best comparison and honor the integrity and value of both. We can learn and benefit from both patterns of behavior.

People who have decided to limit their growing to one or two possibilities for growth have severely restricted their life experience. It feels more like dying than living. By contrast, many people and many congregations draw on all five ways of developing and advancing. The result is that they become a whole, healthy person and grow a strong, healthy congregation.

God shares His grace with us in all five ways. We discover the grace of God in all five of these ways. When we limit ourselves to only one or two of these five, we are limiting our ability to experience the fullness of the grace of God.

Think about one-time, significant experiences with the grace of God. Look in the New Testament. Look back across the history of the Christian movement. Recall the long line of people who have described the pivotal, one-time event that

Offered Possibilities for Growth and How People Discover the Grace of God

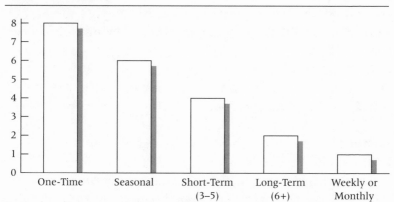

decisively advanced their lives. We have the disciples. We have the woman at the well. We have Paul on the road to Emmaus, Augustine, Martin Luther, Francis of Assisi, and John Wesley. Some of them were following weekly, monthly, year-round practices of the Christian life for a long, long time. In a one-time event, they discovered the grace of God and they became new persons. They were changed forever.

As people share with me about their own day-to-day lives, I am amazed—what they discuss, again and again, are the one-time, decisive events that have shaped their lives for the better. People who have struggled with serious difficulties, over and over, say to me, "This happened on this one day, and my life was changed forever."

We now live in an excellent sprinter culture. Many people discover the grace of God in one-time, seasonal, and short-term events. When it was a marathon culture, the Christian movement learned to plan and behave in a marathon runner spirit. The language of the church communicated with the language of the culture. The culture spoke in a marathon runner language, and the Christian movement spoke in a marathon runner language. We resonated with comparable customs, habits, and traditions found both in the culture and in the Christian movement.

The way of thinking and living in our time, unlike their time, is an excellent sprinter pattern. The language of our time is an excellent sprinter language. The customs, habits, and traditions of our time are of an excellent sprinter nature. We were wise enough to relate to the culture of that earlier time. We are wise enough to relate to the culture of this time. We are wise enough to be open to all five ways in which God comes to us. We will discover the grace, compassion, and hope of God.

5

The Nature of Mission in Our Time

*Lord, when did we see thee hungry and feed thee, or thirsty
and give thee drink?
And when did we see thee a stranger and welcome thee, or
naked and clothe thee?
And when did we see thee sick or in prison and visit thee?*

—MATTHEW 25:37–39

There is a time for grassroots mission. There is a time for top-down mission. This is a time of grassroots mission. In our time, the nature of mission is direct, generous, just enough, and grassroots. We have seen a major paradigm shift from top-down mission to grassroots mission.

Direct Mission

In an earlier time, the emphasis was on an indirect and top-down understanding of the nature of mission. Yes, some mission was direct and grassroots, but the prevailing stress was on a top-down approach. This was buttressed by a theology of the time that tended to be hierarchical in nature. The Christian life was described in hierarchical terms, and elements of the culture reinforced this top-down perspective. In our time, grassroots mission is more effective than top-down mission. Top-down mission is effective. Grassroots mission is more effective.

God gives us a wonderful gift. In this new time, a major possibility for reaching and growing the grass roots is to encourage people to participate in mission that is direct, generous, just enough, and grassroots. A strong, healthy congregation does so. People have a longing to participate in mission of this nature. God's mission is advanced. This congregation reaches and grows the grass roots. People are helped.

The nature of grace shapes the nature of mission. We build our understanding of mission on our understanding of the grace of God:

- God's grace is direct and local, not indirect and remote.
- God's grace is generous, not conserving.
- God's grace is just enough, not too little, not too much, not none at all.
- God's grace is grassroots, not top-down

An effective, healthy congregation offers mission opportunities that live out the nature of God's grace. Grassroots people are stirred in their longings. They participate generously in mission.

In our time, as in all times, people have a compelling longing to serve in mission. This yearning is a gift of God. We are created in the image and likeness of God. God's nature is amazing generosity and grace. God plants within each human heart longings to help. People want their lives to count. They want to share their competencies and compassion in direct, worthwhile mission. They are no longer drawn to mission programs that are indirect and remote, that conserve and hold, that deliver too little or too much help, or none at all, and that are hierarchical in nature. They want to help in direct, generous, just-enough, and grassroots ways.

In an earlier time, people may have been willing for the nature of mission to be more indirect, passed through second, third, and fourth parties. They were content with a conserving approach. They nodded assent to institutional maintenance. They were even willing for the mission to be controlled from the top down. This is no longer the case. Some people continue to do some mission that is indirect and top-down. Increasingly in our time, people want their lives to count directly.

Tip O'Neill once said, "All politics is local." In our recent Christmas letter to family and friends, Julie and I mentioned, along with all the family activities of the year, that our new book, *Small, Strong Congregations,* had just been published. We received a warm note from a longtime friend, Sharon Ulrick, a remarkably wise, gifted person. We count her as family. In her note, she shared her appreciation that the focus of the book is on small, strong congregations. She said, "If all politics is local, all religion must be as well." She shares a helpful thought.

God's grace is direct. God's grace is local. God's grace is not indirect and remote. God is direct and local in sharing grace. God's grace comes directly to you. God sends mentors and saints, encouragers and coaches. God sends guides and leaders, friends and groupings with whom you discover the grace of God. God intends these as "helpers along the way," as Good Samaritans. These people are gifts of God in your life. Moreover, now, in this moment, God's gift to you is this: God's grace is directly, immediately present in your life now, even as you read these words.

God's grace is not remote. A false hierarchy of grace leads to a false hierarchy of institutions. This leads to a false hierarchy of mission. If God had wanted a hierarchy of grace, Jesus would have been born in a mansion or a castle. Any hierarchy of grace is a mirage, used by some as a faint excuse to conceal a hierarchy of institutions. It is illusion. The hierarchies of this world are the feeble creatures of humankind. Some people create these top-down structures; then, desperately, tragically, they try to robe them in God's grace. Distressingly, they try to force and funnel mission only through their top-down structure.

Mission is direct and local because God's grace is direct and local. In our time, people reject a false hierarchy of grace. They know God's grace comes to them directly. They reject a false hierarchy of institutionalism. People join a congregation, not a denomination. They join a movement, not an institution. People are drawn to the congregation nearest their heart, not their house. They want their lives to count—in helpful, serving ways.

People want to participate in direct forms of mission, first-party forms of mission. The mission originates with them and with their local congregation, and their help is directly shared with the people being helped. There is a longing to help directly and personally. We see this in disaster aid teams, long-term relief efforts, Habitat for Humanity, and a multitude of mission projects that local congregations are pursuing directly in their own areas and around the world.

In our time, local means the whole planet. Local no longer means only the immediate neighborhood, or hometown. Most people have a global view of mission, an intergalactic view of the universe. They know our hometown is this planet spinning through the vastness of God's universe. Local means that the mission originates in a local congregation. We have personal ownership for the mission. Local means that we share the mission—personally, directly—in a local area of service and need. We see mission teams both nearby and traveling across the globe to share grace and aid, compassion and help.

The desire of people to participate personally in some mission project is the wellspring of designated giving. It springs from people's longing to share personally in God's mission. Some top-down denominations take the stance that the "upper levels" or the "representative levels" of the denomination know best where mission should be done. In effect they say, "Send your money up to us, and we, in our wisdom, will distribute it, and send it out where we think it is needed. Trust us." People do send money. They do trust. This does not satisfy their longing to participate personally in a mission project that is first-party and direct.

For this reason, they designate some of the mission projects they want their generosity to support. When a top-down denomination discourages designated giving, all that happens is that people send their giving elsewhere. They send it to grassroots groupings that encourage them to designate the mission causes to which they want their generous giving to go. Yes, there is less interest, in our time, in indirect, third-party helping, where the local congregation sends its resources to the denomination, which in turn distributes the help. There is no direct contact with the people being helped. Some people continue to have some interest in giving in this indirect way. They want to do their fair share. People are glad to, are willing to do some of this, but they are drawn compellingly to direct help.

In an earlier time, top-down denominational structures were a useful service in advancing mission. Gathering resources in one place and distributing them elsewhere were important functions. Education of needs was helpful. Training and sending of helping people was useful. Communications and transportation were slow and awkward. A sailing ship, a telegraph line, a horse and wagon, a message delivered by the pony express were all we had. Even as communications and transportation advanced to telephones and trucks, they were still slow.

We live in a new time. The reasons for a top-down gathering of resources, distribution of resources, travel, personnel, communications, and third-party mission structures have disappeared. An array of resources have emerged to help people participate directly in mission. In increasing numbers, people are taking advantage of these new resources. They are sharing in grassroots mission projects around the planet.

In the midst of these advances, there are three growing gaps—at the level of the denomination, the pastors, and the grass roots. The grass roots are God's gift to a congregation. Without the grass roots, there is no congregation. The grass roots give a congregation a sense of life and mission. The grass roots consist of:

- The Easter people. Easter is God's way of teaching us our future. The Easter people are God's sign of the future. They teach us that, if they have a church home, it is here, with us, otherwise on Easter they will be in some other church, or doing something else.

- The Christmas people, who teach us the same.

- People served in mission. These are people helped by this congregation in recent times, through a hospital visit, a wedding, a funeral, and other ways of shepherding.

- Constituents. These people participate in various groupings, programs, and activities of the church. They are informal members and consider themselves part of the family.

- Formal members, on the church roll.

- Friends of the congregation who live elsewhere. They grew up in the congregation, or they were with the congregation for several years. They still consider this congregation home.

- Community people, who think well of the congregation's mission.

These are the grassroots family of the congregation. They both receive and give help, hope, and home. They participate in the sharing and caring of the congregation. They participate in the sacraments of grace, compassion, community, and hope. They are neither informal nor formal key leaders, neither the pastor nor the staff. In a sense, the grass roots include everyone who is not a key leader, pastor, or staff member. They make up the majority of the congregation.

Congregations also have key leaders, a pastor, and sometimes staff. The key leaders are people with formal and/or informal leadership roles. In formal roles, they serve as the chair of the mission committee, the shepherding committee, the worship committee, the giving and finance committee, the trustees, the women's group, and the men's group. In informal roles, the key leaders are people who lead the various significant relational groupings in the congregation—family groupings, vocational groupings, interest groupings, and so on.

Depending on the congregation, the pastor may be a volunteer or paid, part-time or full-time; with some training and credentials or with a seminary degree; and ordained by the congregation, the denomination, or both. The pastor or pastors share the sacraments of mission, shepherding, worship, and leading.

The staff is made up of people who work on specific objectives and perform specific tasks on behalf of the congregation's mission. They may be volunteer or paid, part-time or full-time; depending on the type of congregation, they may have training and credentials. Some are seminary-trained and ordained. Examples include the music director, the church secretary, the custodian, the youth and families director.

There is a gap. Denominational leaders are on one side of the gap. Pastors and key leaders of congregations are on the other side of the gap. There is a second gap. Pastors are on one side of this gap. The key leaders of congregations are on the other side. There is much preoccupation with these two gaps. Considerable time, energy, and effort is invested in discussing and debating the growing gaps between "the denominational leaders and pastors or key leaders" and between "the pastor and the key leaders of the congregation." Retreats are held. Meetings happen regularly. Luncheons occur. Studies are commissioned. Dinners are shared. All of these are concerted efforts to bridge these two gaps with adequate planning, communication, and team building.

There is a third gap. This is the gap between all of these and the grass roots of the local congregation. Denominational leaders, pastors, and key leaders of congregations spend much of their time discussing their own growing gaps. They miss, they fail to see the larger, growing gap, chasm, abyss between them and the grass roots of their congregation.

The new reality is that mission is local, not hierarchical. In an earlier time, it may be that mission was top-down. That way of thinking is no longer persuasive, if indeed it ever was. People who continue to think, act, and behave that way are disappointed. This enormous, growing gap is part of a larger phenomenon that is pervasive in the whole of the culture. Similar immense, growing gaps are happening in the political and economic spheres of life. Business, vocational, civic, community, educational, and recreation circles are experiencing the same growing chasm.

In all of these spheres of life, people have become disenchanted. No, that is too easy a word. They have given up on top-down, hierarchical approaches to life. Such top-down approaches to life have promised, and promised, and promised. They did not deliver. The old notion was, "Be loyal to the company, and the company will be loyal to you." What people now understand is, "Be loyal to the company and the company will not be loyal to you."

The new reality is direct mission. The new reality is more than despair and disappointment, more than distress and disillusionment with top-down, hierarchical approaches. It is simply that these approaches no longer have any drawing power. Grassroots people no longer see any compelling value in such an approach. It is not that they are angry at those approaches. At least if they were angry, they would still be paying attention. No, it is more profound. With a shrug of their shoulders, they just walk away. It is not even apathy. It is not that they no longer care. It is more serious. They have simply concluded that those top-down approaches no longer have any commanding resonance with their lives.

Thus an increasing number of people search out, look for, and long to be part of some group, where they can serve in mission directly. They want to see the immediate consequences of their serving. They want some group that is family and community. They want some group where there are not layers of committees and structures. They know life is short. They want to be part of some group that does not take forever to make a simple decision for mission. They do not want to be placated and ignored. They want some group where, when they suggest an idea for mission, people listen to what they suggest.

Denominational leaders, pastors, and key leaders are so preoccupied with their own gaps that they do not listen. They miss the growing gap between them and the grass roots. The consequence is that the grass roots look elsewhere to participate in mission. They discover community groups, civic groups, educational groups, service groups, vocational groups, recreational groups, interest groups, and so forth, wherein they can live out and fulfill their longings to serve in mission. They create new groupings to do so. They live out the nature of mission in their personal and family lives.

In many congregations, little happens to close this growing gap, to reach the grass roots. The knock on the grass roots is that they are not "really committed." It may be the case that the grass roots are not committed to some of the pet projects of the key leaders and pastors, or of some top-down structure. The grass roots are committed to mission projects they help decide and in which they can participate directly. The commitment excuse, invented by some pastors and key leaders, is a convenient device they use so they do not have to fool with the grass roots.

A weak, declining, or dying congregation makes some vague attempt once or twice a year to enlist the grass roots to serve on committees of the church, to teach in the Sunday school, or to help in the office. What passes for a volunteer recruitment program is an effort to get the grass roots to do what the church wants them to do. The focus is on filling the various committee slots of the organizational structure. The effort is to get someone to do what the structure needs help with. These attempts have a top-down orientation.

In an effective congregation, the volunteer programs are an effort to discover what the grass roots want to do, and discover the mission projects with which they would like to help. In a weak, declining, or dying congregation, there is rarely any attempt to invite the thinking and wisdom, the excellent ideas and good suggestions of the grass roots. Indeed, the grass roots are viewed with some halting suspicion, primarily because—to the key leaders, pastor, and staff—the grass roots represent the unknown.

A healthy congregation views the grass roots as central. The leaders and pastors, with an active, encouraging spirit, invite the thinking, wisdom, excellent ideas, and good suggestions of the grass roots. They focus on helping the grass roots discover their gifts and competencies, and on matching their strengths with their longings to help. The spirit is, "We are in this together. We discover mission and service together. We discover how to live whole, healthy lives. Gathered in the grace of God, we listen to one another. We learn with one another. We value one another. We share direct mission. We are God's own people."

Generous Mission

God's grace is generous. Mission is generous because God's grace is generous. Mission is not conserving and holding, protecting and preserving. God's grace is spontaneous. Mission is spontaneous because God's grace is spontaneous. God's grace is natural. It is in the nature of God to share His grace. Mission is natural and spontaneous, not forced and artificial. Mission is spontaneous generosity. It is in our nature to share in mission. Mission is as natural as breathing.

We are created in the image and likeness of God. Our true nature is to be generous. Whenever we find a person who is stingy and selfish, most times we have found a person who is scared or scarred by life. He or she is using stingy and selfish as self-protective mechanisms to protect himself or herself from being scared and scarred yet another time. We live forward to our best, true selves as we share mission.

Mission is generous, spontaneous, and natural. Mission is the stirring of gentle, generous gestures of grace and compassion, community and hope. Most times, these gestures of kindness are shared with a spirit of natural, spontaneous generosity. We discover this spirit of mission in the twenty-fifth chapter of the Gospel of Matthew, verses 21–46. The text has to do with the Last Judgment. The key is in the verses I presented at the beginning of this chapter: "Then the righteous will answer Him, Lord, when did we see thee hungry and feed thee, or thirsty and give thee drink? And when did we see thee a stranger and welcome thee, or naked and clothe thee? And when did we see thee sick or in prison and visit thee?"

They are puzzled. Surprised. Amazed. They do not quite understand. There is a sense of wonderment in their questions.

Many have commented that the whole passage, verses 21–46, suggests the qualities of the Christian life. Those who live out these qualities will enter into eternal life. Those who do not live out these qualities will not. Sermons have been preached. Bible studies have been held. The message has been "If you want to enter into eternal life, then these are the qualities important for you to live out in this life." Sometimes, the sermons have been more law than grace. The message has been, "You must do these things. You should do these. You ought to do these."

The key to understanding the text is this: those who are selected as the righteous are unaware they were living out these qualities in their daily lives. They were doing what came generously and naturally to them. They were sharing acts of spontaneous grace and generosity, mercy, and kindness. To be sure, some mission is planned, proactive, and intentional. Indeed in recent times, I have come to the thought that we do mission planning to learn the spirit of mission, and eventually we discover the spontaneity of mission.

I was watching one of the Final Four teams in college basketball. This is an excellent team, but they were down twenty-two points by halftime. During the third and fourth quarters, they came, amazingly, from behind and won by eleven points. The point swing was thirty-three points during the second half of the game, mostly in the fourth quarter. Later, a reporter asked the coach what he told the players during halftime. The coach said he told them, "Forget the plays, play basketball, have fun." The team had become too preoccupied with the plays. They discovered, in the second half, the spontaneity and naturalness of the game.

Mission is a way of life. People who share mission are not self-conscious about their helping. They are hardly aware it is happening. They are simply being who they are. When commended, they are surprised. With a spirit of spontaneous generosity, they share gentle, generous gestures of mission, kindness, compassion, and mercy. They have not consciously been "doing mission." It is in their nature. The Good Samaritan does what is generous, spontaneous, and natural. For the priest and the Levite, the man by the side of the road was not in their mission plan.

I met Don and Linda at a seminar that I was leading. The sponsors of the seminar wanted them to meet me. I wanted to meet them. Prior to the seminar, I had learned they are legends for their mission work both in this country and in South America. As we visited together over lunch, they shared their story with me.

One Sunday, as they sat in church listening to their pastor's sermon, something stirred in both their hearts. After the service, they shared with one another that each wanted to help in some mission. Don is a graduate of a major medical school and is considered one of the leading experts in internal medicine in his own state and is known throughout the country. Linda is a graduate of a major medical school. Her field is pediatrics. She has an amazing gift for working with mothers and children. Both of them decided that they wanted to use their training and competencies doing short-term mission projects during the summer.

They wrote to the national missions office of their denomination. Several weeks passed. They did not hear back. They decided to call. They were passed from one person to the next. Finally, the fifth person they talked to said, "Sure, I'll be glad to help you. I'll send you the application forms." They were good-natured about the routine and the process. Several more weeks passed. The forms finally arrived—a stack more than an inch thick for each of them. Understanding policies and procedures, they completed and mailed the forms.

They waited.

They did not hear a single word. Several months passed. Again, they phoned the office. They learned the filled-out forms had arrived. Don and Linda suggested they would fly, at their own expense, to the national headquarters. They worked out an appointment time to see the proper person. They flew a day early to be sure they would make their appointment the next day. They arrived for the appointment and learned that the person they were to see was out having coffee. They waited. Finally, the person returned. He seemed to be in a hurry. They had come a long way, on their own money. He met with them briefly. He told them, "I will be in touch. We can use your help."

Weeks passed. No word. Nothing happened.

One day, Don was talking by telephone to a good friend, a doctor in a state on the other side of the country. They had graduated from medical school together. Don shared with him their longings to help in mission. He talked about their frustration with the lack of response from the denomination's mission office, and the fact that there seemed to be little interest in using their time and competencies.

His friend said, "I go to South America each summer for four weeks. You and Linda can come with me and be part of our team. Several doctors and nurses go; a number of support people complete our team. We would appreciate your help. Can you go with us next summer?" Don and Linda leaped at the opportunity.

Time has passed. They are legends for their volunteer mission work in that part of South America.

The story is told of a child who was always late coming home from school. School was out at three o'clock. It was a short walk from the school to their house. She should be home by 3:15. In fact, she came in at a variety of times. Every day the time varied. One day, her mother asked, "Why is it that you are always late getting home from school and the time is so irregular?" The child answered, "It's our school crossing guard." "What do you mean?" the mother asked. The little girl explained, "At the corner where she helps us cross the street, she waits until some cars come, so she can hold up her sign and stop the cars while she takes us across the street. Until some cars come along, we have to wait."

Don, Linda, and I reflected on their experience with their denomination. In a way, the people at national headquarters had spent much effort in trying to cajole people into doing mission, without much success. They were simply not prepared to deal with Don and Linda's generosity and willingness to share in mission with a spontaneous, natural spirit. Headquarters had a slow, weary timetable. Now, Don and Linda had a timetable. They hoped to go the following summer or the summer after that. They could not just up and leave their active medical practices. However, national headquarters could think only in years, and in slow, careful, slow (yes, the word is intended to be here twice), routine, procedural ways.

Policies and procedures, rules and regulations, conditions and stipulations are appropriate. They help to ensure that no misfit gets to the mission field, at home or abroad. Too many rules block healthy people. The intent of the many regulations is to block one misfit from getting to a mission project, but the multiplicity of rules discourages many healthy people from participating in the mission.

I am not suggesting there be no rules. I do suggest there be fewer regulations. Yes, some misfit may get to a mission. The healthy people who get there will outnumber them. It is amazing how rules breed and multiply. They become a collection of exceptions. An exception arises one time, and someone creates a new regulation. Healthy policies cover the general rule of thumb, not the exceptions. Healthy groups review their policies regularly. They want to prevent their policies and procedures manual from becoming a collection of exceptions.

In a spirit of spontaneous generosity, Don and Linda simply wanted to help in mission. Their credentials are impeccable. The character and quality of their life is healthy and wholesome. They are active, contributing members of their community and their congregation. Through a friend, they did finally discover a way in which they could share their generosity in mission. As I listened to their story, I wondered how many people had been through similar experiences. I wondered how many competent, compassionate people have had to find their own way because some structure was slow to respond.

I have the privilege of visiting with people around the world. I am deeply impressed with the multitudes of people who live life with a spirit of spontaneous generosity, mercy, and kindness. They do not even know they are doing mission. It is simply who they are, and whose they are. The results of their generosity are legendary. Whether it is a housewife or a ditch digger, a salesperson or a biology teacher, a person who works in a hospital, a food server in a restaurant, or another who travels across the regions of our country, in whatever walk or way of life, countless people share their generosity in helpful acts of kindness.

Likewise, a strong, effective congregation shares mission with a generous, spontaneous spirit. It is not a matter of whether it is in the plan. It is not a matter of whether the congregation has the resources. It is simply a case where the hungry are fed, the thirsty are given drink, strangers are welcomed as part of the family, those who need clothing are clothed, the sick are visited, and those in prison are helped. Healthy congregations know this: God is generous with us. We are generous with the people God gives us to serve in mission.

Just Enough Help in Mission

A sweet silence had settled across the land. The cooling evening breezes were like a welcoming friend. It had been a long, hard day. There were many travelers on the road. The inn was full. His grandfather had started the inn. His father had enlarged the kitchen. He had built the business.

Two window shutters to close, three candles to snuff, and it would be time to go to bed. A faint knock on the door, barely heard. It came again. Who could that be at this time of night? He went slowly to the door and opened it.

A man stood before him. The man was dressed like a Samaritan. Behind him stood a donkey with a rumpled clump of clothing on its back. The pile of clothing slipped slowly to the ground as the innkeeper watched. Then, from the ground came a moan. The Samaritan told the innkeeper that he had found the man by the side of the road, beaten and robbed, and that he had brought him to the inn for help. Could the innkeeper help?

It is interesting to think of the possibilities available to the innkeeper. He could have said, "There is no room in the inn. I cannot help." He could have taken the man in, taken advantage of the Samaritan's generosity, and given more help than was really needed. The Samaritan had said, "Whatever it costs, I will pay you on my return." The innkeeper could have seen his dream of a condominium on the Sea of Galilee finally coming true. The innkeeper chose neither of these alternatives.

What the innkeeper did was to take the man in and help him just enough so that he could be on his way. There is nothing in the text that suggests the innkeeper delivered so much help that, out of gratitude and gratefulness, the beaten and robbed man lived out the rest of his days with the innkeeper. That would have been a dependent-codependent pattern of behavior.

In the parable, the priest passes by on the other side of the road. I sometimes imagine that he might have been on his way to a church-growth conference; helping the man would not have fit into his church-growth plan. Likewise, the Levite passes by on the other side of the road. I sometimes imagine that he does so simply because the beaten and robbed man does not fit into the policies and procedures, conditions and stipulations, rules and regulations of how the Levite thinks help should be given.

The genius of the parable is that the passerby least likely to stop, the Samaritan, was the one who did stop. There is nothing in the parable that suggests he first ponders, thinks, considers, and weighs the consequences. For him, it is simply a generous, spontaneous act of kindness. What the Samaritan does is get the man to the inn. What the innkeeper does is give the man just enough help that he can be on his way. The two pivotal figures in the parable are the Samaritan and the innkeeper. Both of them deliver just enough help that the man can continue his journey.

We learn this from the parable. God delivers just enough help to us so that we can be on our journey. Sometimes, God comes in the form of a Samaritan, sometimes in the form of an innkeeper. What God does is share with us acts of spontaneous generosity, kindness, and grace, so that we can be on our journey through this life.

What we learn is that the art of helping is to deliver just enough help to be helpful, but not so much help that the help becomes harmful and creates a pattern of dependency-codependency. Some people deliver no help. They pass by on the other side of the road. Some people deliver too much help. Their eagerness to be helpful takes hold of them. Their desire to be a helping person gets the best of them. Their compulsive perfectionism takes hold. They deliver more help than would be helpful.

Some congregations deliver too much help. The pendulum swings. They deliver no help. The pendulum swings. They deliver too little help. They deliver conserving help. They want to hold onto their meager resources. They give out of a conserving and holding, protecting and preserving spirit, not out of a spirit of generosity. The pendulum swings. They overcompensate and deliver too much help.

An effective congregation, with a high density of whole, healthy people, gives just enough help. Sometimes, the way forward in a weak, declining, or dying congregation is to grow the health of the people in the congregation forward. As a consequence, the health of the congregation advances. Healthy people and healthy congregations deliver just enough help.

We learn this from the parable. The Samaritan takes no thought for himself. The innkeeper takes no thought for himself. The focus is on helping the man who has been beaten and robbed. Healthy congregations are like this. They take no thought for any payoff for the congregation. Their interest is in the people they serve in mission, whether the people are in the congregation, in the community, or on the other side of the planet. They do the mission for the sake of the mission.

An unhealthy congregation is concerned primarily with membership. It does the mission, if at all, for the sake of members. They ask, "Will this grow a bigger church?" Less blatantly, they ask, "What is in it for us?" Their annual meetings are filled with talk about whether their membership has increased or decreased. They barely discuss, with even mild interest, the number of people they have helped, or the number who have discovered Christ in the preceding year. Their preoccupation is a self-serving, institutional focus on membership.

I greatly admire the Salvation Army. They focus on the total people they have served in mission in recent years. They pray and plan, help and serve people in the current year. They look forward to the coming year—and the total people they will have the privilege of serving in mission. They keep statistics on the people served in mission. Their theology of statistics reveals a theology of serving. Some other congregations' and denominations' theology of statistics reveals a theology of surviving. The Salvation Army does the mission for the integrity of the mission. The Samaritan and the innkeeper take no thought of what is in it for them. They help—generously, spontaneously, naturally—and they deliver just enough help.

God invites us to share such a mission in the world. Our mission, as a congregation, is not, finally, in getting a bigger membership. Our mission is richer, more profound than that. Our mission is serving people in the world, helping them with their human hurts and hopes, their life stages, their strengths and their weaknesses, their growing and developing, and their own mission in serving. We deliver just enough help that they can be on their journey in this life and can be a part of the mission team.

In working with congregations, I find this table helpful. We can share help in one-time, seasonal, short-term, long-term, and weekly or monthly ways. The New Testament is filled with events in which Jesus delivers one-time help. The art of being a healthy congregation is delivering just enough help and doing so in a way that fits the need. In a given situation, ask yourself, "What way of sharing help will fit this need?"

The Samaritan, I sometimes think, is an excellent sprinter. Likewise, I think the innkeeper is an excellent sprinter. Both of them have the wisdom to deliver the help that is appropriate and important for the moment, so that the wounded man

How to Share Help

	One-Time	Seasonal	Short-Term	Long-Term	Weekly or Monthly
Food					
Clothing					
Shelter					
Work					
Prayer					
Visiting					
Motivation, inspiration					
Education, information					
Fellowship, sharing					
Support, caring					
Referral, resources					
Crisis intervention					
Intensive					
Other possibilities					

can be on his journey. The Samaritan and the innkeeper deliver one-time help. For his one-time act of generosity, the Samaritan, in the centuries come and gone, has been called the Good Samaritan. Sometimes I think that the priest and the Levite were solid marathon runners, and the only way they could envision helping someone was in long-term or weekly, monthly, year-round ways. It was clear to the Samaritan and the innkeeper that the man beaten and robbed was simply in need of a one-time act of spontaneous generosity and kindness.

The nature of mission in our time is to deliver just enough help—with wisdom and compassion, vision and common sense. Healthy mission is able to have no interest in developing dependent-codependent patterns of behavior. Healthy mission is able to deliver just enough help—consistently. Some people are inconsistent. They pass by on the other side of the road and give no help, and then later they overcompensate because they feel guilty and deliver too much help to be helpful and the help becomes harmful. Then they deliver too little help. A pattern of no help, too much, too little help is a series of pendulum swings to avoid. God invites us to share help in the way that God shares His grace with us. God shares just enough help that we can be on our journey in this life.

Grassroots Mission

God's grace is grassroots. Mission is grassroots because God's grace is grassroots. God's grace is not top-down. Mission is not top-down. Mission is serving and encouraging, not controlling and dominating. The nature of mission in our time is grassroots. God invites us to be part of a grassroots movement in one of the richest ages for mission the Christian movement has ever known. God shares this generous invitation with all of humanity.

Our God is the God of the grass roots. God is the source of grace. God chooses to share grace with whomsoever God decides. God's grace is the compelling influence; the center of a whole, healthy life; and the originating source of mission. God's reforming acts of grace touch the whole of humanity directly. In dealing with humankind, God acts straightforwardly, with immediacy, and with the everyday grassroots people of the time. God has compelling interest in grassroots movements that share mission.

Grace is grassroots.

God does not limit God's grace only to what humankind has created. God does not share grace solely through the inventions of humankind. God is not interested in institutions that become preoccupied with their own welfare, prestige, and power. God invites the structures of humankind to service and mission, humility and caring, not ruling and controlling, not power and maintenance.

In the course of time, humankind has tried various structures to serve and care for humanity, and to do so with a spirit of humility and a sense of mission. We have tried state, church, and business possibilities. Each was an interesting effort to be a compelling influence; a center for a whole, healthy life; and an originating source of mission to serve humankind. When these structures are serving and caring, with humility and mission, for the sake of humankind, there are three consequences:

1. God supports the venture with His grace.
2. The venture is compelling with the grass roots.
3. Humanity is helped.

Whenever a structure becomes preoccupied with its own welfare—with ruling, controlling, power, and maintenance—then God withdraws the support of His grace, and that venture no longer has compelling value with the grass roots. No structure can survive without the grace of God and the consent of the grass roots. The grass roots decide that a certain structure is a pleasant irrelevancy and has no helpful bearing on their lives. It simply becomes ineffectual, grinds to a halt, no longer works. The venture withers and is dust.

The Roman empire was a structure of humankind. Some suggest that its earliest beginnings seem to have been of a serving nature. Time passed. The state became an empire. It became the controlling influence, the center of power, the focus of life, and originating source of action. "Rome is eternal" was the banner to which armies marched, merchants sailed, roads were built, and people were ruled. For all its vastness, and its seemingly impervious nature, Rome, with its abuses and corruption, fell.

In the midst of that vast empire, the Christian movement was born in a manger. It was God's intention that Jesus be born in a manger, not a mansion; in a cattle stall, not a castle; in a stable, not a stronghold. The manger is God's sign that God shares His grace with the whole of humanity, not simply with or through kings and emperors.

In the East, the empire lasted another thousand years, and an interesting convergence of state and church emerged. The church grew in ascendancy as it aligned itself with the remains of the empire. Further to the north and east, it aligned itself with the emperors of Russia and gained power—power such as the world confers and bestows. However, that finally gave way.

In the West, the notion emerged that the City of Man was the invention and creation of man, and this was why Rome fell. Augustine affirmed that all kingdoms rise and fall, all civilizations come and go. With Augustine, the notion emerged that the City of God is the invention of God, and it therefore will not fail. Some, however, equated the City of God with the church.

With the fall of Rome in 410 A.D., the church, particularly in the West, became a rallying point for humanity. The focus shifted from the state to the church as the center of life. It became the primary moving force in Western civilization. It became the controlling influence, the center of power, and the originating source of mission to serve humankind. The church grew in power and prestige, influence and authority, command and control.

Under the banner of the church, armies marched, merchants sailed, roads were built, and people were ruled. The church became preoccupied with its own power. It lost the spirit of serving and caring. It forgot humility and mission. It focused on ruling, controlling, and institutional maintenance. The

Roman empire had its share of abuses and corruption. As time passed, the church, in both the West and the East, revealed its own frailties, abuses, corruption, and preoccupation with its own survival and welfare.

Amidst the failings of the church, the nation states of Europe arose as an alternative structure. A contest emerged as to which—church or state—would be the focus of life, the controlling influence, and the source of serving humankind. Several solutions emerged:

- The state is the primary source of serving humanity, in any of its configurations, now or in the past.
- The church, with an institutional, hierarchical orientation, is the primary source of serving humanity.
- The church-state relationship, with the church dominating the state in many areas, leaves some matters to the state to control.
- The state-church relationship, with the state dominating the church in many areas, leaves some matters to the church to control.
- Separation of church and state is in the belief that each has its proper and separate realm of activity and influence in serving humankind.
- Business, wherein state-church struggles are bypassed, focuses on what business can contribute to the well-being of humanity.

Each of these solutions has contributed its own strengths and advantages. Each did some good work for humankind and was helpful in some ways. In the end, none of these solutions has worked. The abuses and corruption of each is part of the reason they have not worked. Ultimately, they fail because they become top-down, institutional solutions. Thus they are not able to sustain the compelling, lasting interest of the grass roots. They become bureaucratic, organizational, hierarchical efforts. They assume the focus of life, the controlling influence, the center of power; the originating source of serving and mission is in some top-down, institutional structure.

In each, the fatal assumption is a hierarchy of grace and power that is to be passed down from the institution to the grass roots. The struggles between the state and the church—about who should be top and who should be down in ruling, controlling, and institutional maintenance—have gone on for a long, long time. So long that humanity is weary and disillusioned with any such hierarchical solutions.

In the midst of this historical disillusionment, a few proposed a notion that "God would reform the church, and then the church would reform the culture." This false, fragile sentiment, however, was simply a latent archeological relic of an old, feeble hypothesis that God relates to the church and the church relates to the world. God does not limit His grace. It is not that God reforms the church and then the church reforms the culture. God deals directly with the whole of humankind.

The manger, the life, the teachings, the upper room, the cross, the open tomb—these are all signs that God deals directly with the whole of humanity.

In the nineteenth century, given the disillusionment with both state and church solutions, a few proposed the notion that business, in the form of megacompanies, would be the way forward. Business would supersede the nation states with their fragile bickering and petty alliances. Business would supersede the church, with its own baggage and abuses. Business would bypass the struggles between the state and the church. Now, this was not a new proposal. In some ancient times, businesses had a comparable scale of size, wealth, and power as in the present day, and they postured themselves as the way forward.

Nevertheless, in the latter part of the nineteenth century, the idea emerged again. In a humane, helpful manner, business would be the focus of life and the originating source of serving humankind. The first mill towns, at their humane best, were efforts in this direction. These early efforts by business to better humanity looked promising. However, the robber baron companies committed many abuses and much self-serving profanation. This caused a reaction against business and a return to the state as the primary source of bettering humankind. The middle of the twentieth century saw the shift from robber barons to the state. Since then, in some quarters, there has been a shift back to business because of the inefficiency, corruption, and abuse of the state.

In their beginnings, in whatever various configurations they emerge, the structures of state, church, and business give indication of their desire to serve humanity, to be in touch with the grass roots. Each is aware, however dimly, of its need to have the compelling interest and lasting support of the grass roots. Each, in its distinctive way, seeks to be in conversation with the grass roots. Each has the sense that, if it loses contact with the grass roots, then its ability to survive, let alone thrive, is in jeopardy.

The state, as a dictatorial empire, does not work. It quickly loses contact with the grass roots (if it ever has it). The state, as a democracy, comes closer to working. It has about it the spirit of focusing on the grass roots. At its best, a democracy knows the grass roots are the controlling influence and the center of power. However, whenever the bureaucracy of a democratic state loses touch with the grass roots and acts in heavy-handed, top-down ways, even that democracy risks losing the compelling interest of the grass roots. Whenever a democracy stays closely in touch with the grass roots, it thrives and flourishes and benefits humankind.

The church, as a structural entity, works whenever it serves humanity with humility and mission. A church structure does not work whenever it becomes preoccupied with its own status and power and behaves in a top-down, hierarchical manner. In earlier times, the church had the benefit of the monastic movements. These were efforts by the grass roots to serve in mission, to halt the institutionalization of the church, and to call the church back to its spirit of being a grassroots mission. In the twentieth century, Pope John XXIII sought to lead the Roman Catholic church closer to the grass roots. In recent times, we have seen the emergence of hosts of grassroots movements to do the same.

With an encouraging spirit, the Mission Growth Movement is a grassroots movement with a compelling focus on mission. Some current reform efforts within certain denominations seek to do the same. In a certain sense, the megacongregation is a minimovement within a denomination to advance the cause of reaching the grass roots. Significantly, the movement of small, strong congregations seeks to be a healthy, grassroots effort.

In business and industry, much is made of MBWA, that is, management by walking around. The emphasis is on the manager being present on the factory floor, out in the work areas, in touch with the employees of the company. The driving force of this approach is to avoid a top-down understanding of management, and to see management as grassroots in its orientation. Whenever a manager stays closely in touch with the grass roots, the business flourishes.

Insofar as the state, the church, or business thinks and plans, behaves and lives with a compelling interest in the grass roots, then each has viability and compelling value. Whenever each thinks, plans, behaves, acts, and lives as a top-down institution, with its focus on self-serving maintenance and on its own prestige and power, then each has a dim, fleeting future.

Each of these solutions seeks to wrestle with the dilemma of which organizing principle serves and strengthens humanity. They do good work. They fail. None has staying power, enduring stability, and lasting strength. None is finally compelling. Each works for a time. Then the leaders make the mistake of assuming the venture is all their own doing, that they are the source of authority, power, and control. They lose sight of the grace and power of God. They trust their current structure and themselves as being the answer. They become top-down. Power corrupts? No. People corrupt themselves. It is not the fault of power, as some outside, insidious force. People choose to corrupt themselves.

State, church, and business each has value, purpose, and significance. Each is helpful and appropriate. Each has its season, its time, its day. Each is a useful way forward at a given point in the evolving adventure of humanity. What happens? What are the danger signals? Take notice of these clues:

- When man makes absolute what God sees as relative, the approach withers and decays.

- When man makes static what God sees as dynamic, the approach withers and decays.

- When man makes central what God sees as simply useful for the moment, the approach withers and decays.

- When man makes "to be served" what God sees as "there to be serving," then the approach withers and decays.

In our time, perhaps in all times but certainly in our time, we are drawn to grassroots movements that share mission, not top-down institutions that focus on maintenance. These grassroots movements see themselves as

- Relative, not absolute
- Dynamic, not static
- For the moment, useful, not central
- Serving, not being served

We stay grassroots. We do not become top-down. We know God's grace is grassroots, not top-down. We focus on serving and caring, humility and mission.

We know God is the source of grace. We live with the confidence that God chooses to share grace directly with humanity. We know God's grace is the compelling influence; the center of a whole, healthy life; and the originating source of mission that leads us on the journey of this life. We seek to contribute value in the ongoing, developing saga of humanity. We want our lives to count in some tangible, worthwhile way. We want to be part of a grassroots movement, living in the grace of God that serves well in mission.

God is direct. God is generous. God shares just enough help to be helpful, so that we can be on the journey of this life. God is grassroots. In all times, and especially in our time, the nature of mission matches the nature of God. We are the Christian movement, not the Christian institution. There is a time for state, church, or business. We live with humility and gratitude in the grace of God. This is the time for mission—direct, generous, sharing just enough help, and grassroots in spirit.

6

Creativity and Objectives

I came that they might have life, and have it abundantly.

—JOHN 10:10

Creativity and objectives are good friends. They go together. Creativity gives wings to our objectives. Objectives give feet to our creativity. Creativity without objectives is confusion— disarray, a muddle that goes nowhere. Objectives without creativity have a dull, dreary sameness, and likewise go nowhere. Each gives life to the other. There is a wonderful dynamic between the two. It is hard to know which gives rise to the other. Sometimes, our spontaneous creativity leads us to a specific objective. Sometimes, the yearning to achieve a certain objective stirs our best creativity.

There is a time for creativity and objectives. There is a time for controlling and directing. This is a time for creativity and objectives. In our time, people are drawn to congregations that encourage their creativity rather than to institutions that seek to direct them. People are drawn to congregations that help them achieve objectives they decide to pursue and for which they have ownership rather than institutions that control what they should do.

Ways of Learning

One possibility God gives us for reaching and growing the grass roots is to encourage creativity and objectives. A healthy congregation does this. It encourages people's creativity. It helps them achieve objectives for which they have owner-ship. It does not control and direct what they should do. An effective, healthy congregation helps people:

- Advance their ways of learning
- Develop the signs of creativity
- Focus on objectives that are creative and have value
- Accomplish specific, concrete objectives

A healthy congregation encourages people to advance their ways of learning. We learn in a remarkable variety of ways. The art is to stir and advance as many ways of learning as possible. We can cultivate and develop multiple ways of learning. We learn to learn. An effective congregation offers a rich range of learning possibilities. The result is that we dis-cover and grow many ways of learning forward, to help us live a whole, healthy life in the grace of God.

Years ago, Julie and I shared a wonderful retreat with a group of youths. On a cool, crisp October weekend, we gath-ered at a quiet, inspiring site. The camp was filled with tall, stately, ancient trees, their leaves turned brilliant autumn colors. Around the campfire on Friday evening, we began to talk about what it is like to be in high school. Our conversa-tion continued on Saturday. We explored a range of possibil-ities that young people discover in high school. We talked further on Sunday, concluding with a service of worship and prayer, that the grace of God would lead us in the days and weeks to come.

A short time later, I was reflecting on the retreat. I came to what I call discovery number one: the major cultural groupings of a high school. These are the cultural groupings teens discover and become a part of during their years in secondary school:

- Athletic
- Intellectual
- Extracurricular
- Social
- Fad of the moment
- Outcast
- Independent

These cultural groupings are pervasively present in most high schools. We can open a yearbook and see the groupings. We may see slightly more pictures of the extracurricular grouping than of the others. The extracurricular cultural grouping produces the yearbook. Hence, almost without knowing it, they put in more pictures of the clubs and activity groups that make up their extracurricular culture.

Various others may develop in an individual school. Since my early reflections on our retreat, I have discovered that a high school sometimes has:

- A variety of ethnic groups
- Alcohol and drug groups, with one or both of these as their primary link and tie
- Gang groups, who develop a distinct culture, philosophy, and practice of living
- Interest groups, whose primary focus is on some activity outside of school

- Immigrant groups, specifically first-, second-, and third-generation

- Single parents, who are seeking to finish school and at the same time raise a child or children

- Youths who are working to support themselves and their family

On occasion, the last two go together.

Sometimes, these high school groupings extend into adult life. In many congregations, I visit an adult Sunday school class called the fellowship class. I know I am in the social grouping. When I visit the workers class, I know I am in the extracurricular, work project grouping. I visit the Kerygma class. I know I am in the intellectual grouping (the members are the only ones who can remember how to spell the name!). I once walked into a Sunday school class, and they said to me, in a friendly, happy, good natured spirit, "Dr. Callahan, we want you to know that we're the class that's against most everything in this church." I knew I was in the outcast class.

Time passed. I discovered more and more about the cultural groupings in high school. I found that, in our time, they extend into junior high and middle school and into the older elementary grades. I began to think about the life pattern present in each grouping. This led me to what I call discovery number two: the distinctive qualities of each cultural grouping. Each cultural grouping develops distinctive:

- Goals and values
- Customs, habits, and traditions
- Language and communications networks
- Leadership and processes for making decisions
- Sacred places of meeting
- A common shared vision of the future

Sometimes, there is overlap between these cultural groupings. Some groupings may develop similar traits. There is interchange. A youth will be in one grouping and at some point during the high school days he or she will move to another grouping. There is multiple membership. Some youths are able to bring off active participation in more than one cultural grouping and to sustain their multiple memberships throughout their high school days.

The smaller the high school, the more likely overlap, interchange, and multiple membership are to happen. The larger the high school, the less likely overlap, interchange, and multiple membership are taking place, and the more distinct and separate the cultural groupings remain.

We reach people where they are, not where we think they should be, or where we wish they were. I have, I think, always known this. Once I began to understand the cultural groupings of a high school and the distinctive qualities of each, this led me to discovery number three: foundational principles for reaching youth. Two principles contribute to building a strong, healthy mission with young people:

• We develop programs and activities that match the specific grouping we hope to help. For example, a ski trip, a basketball team, or a baseball team reaches the athletic grouping. An intensive Bible study retreat reaches the intellectual grouping. A Friday night party reaches the social grouping. Some youths come to all three because they see "their turn is coming." Many youths come to the one that resonates with them.

• We offer these possibilities with an excellent sprinter and solid marathon runner balance. In our time, I encourage you to offer many one-time, seasonal, and short-term opportunities. You will reach both excellent sprinters and solid marathon runners. You can offer several long-term and weekly or monthly possibilities to reach primarily solid marathon runners.

I share this "youth mission" chart with many congregations.

Possibilities for Reaching Young People

	One-Time	Seasonal	Short-Term (3–5)	Long-Term (6+)	Weekly, Monthly, Year-Round
Athletic					
Intellectual					
Extracurricular					
Social					
Fad of the moment					
Outcast					
Independent					
Various, school to school					

The test of an active youth program is the total number of young people being reached during the year. The test is not how many show up for the youth group on Sunday evening. We will reach youths in one-time, seasonal, short-term, long-term, and weekly or monthly events that have a specific focus with specific cultural groupings within the whole of the youth culture. The test of a youth program is the extent to which we are helping these youths advance their lives and shape their destinies in the grace of God.

In many small, strong congregations, there simply are not the leadership resources to have a Sunday evening youth group that meets weekly, monthly, year-round, every Sunday night. What they do, extraordinarily, creatively, is hold one-time, seasonal, and short-term events, projects, and activities that touch the lives of many youths in the congregation and in the community. Consequently, these small, strong congregations have some of the most active youth programs in their communities.

We are wise enough to know that adults come in different sizes and shapes; that is, they have distinctive interests and relational networks. One adult grouping gathers around an interest in athletics. Another gathers around an intellectual interest in thoughtful Bible study. Another group likes to do work projects (extracurricular). Yet another grouping likes to participate in social, relational activities. Yes, overlap, interchange, and multiple membership take place. At the same time, we have a variety of adult groupings in a congregation. This is a normal pattern with adults.

The only people who try to collapse all youths into one grouping on Sunday night are adults. We are wise enough to not announce, on a given Sunday, that, henceforth, all adult Sunday school classes will be merged into one class. We know that this does not work—and this is with adults. If we know it does not work with adults, why would we think that it would work with young people?

When we try to collapse all of them into one Sunday night youth group, mostly, the result is that we reach either the extracurricular or the social group. We may reach one or two youths from the other cultural groupings—regrettably, just few enough to create an illusion that one group can reach all youths. We honor the distinctive interests of adults. Healthy congregations do the same with young people. We offer a rich variety of possibilities and we reach and help many youths with their lives, in the grace of God.

In the time come and gone since that remarkable youth retreat, I have learned much about people, and the pace and the ways of learning with which God blesses us. My research and my wisdom led me to what I call discovery number four: the pace at which people learn. We discussed this in the chapter on the cultural shift to excellent sprinters. I came to this discovery as I was in the process of thinking through how, in our time, one might share a mission with youth.

I discovered that young people, indeed, all people, learn in one-time, seasonal, short-term, long-term, and weekly or monthly ways. We learn as excellent sprinters and as solid marathon runners. We respond the way we do to information, materials, and structures because that is the pace at which we have learned to learn. We can learn to learn at all of these paces, and in a given setting we can decide which pace of learning works best.

In recent times, I have come to what I call discovery number five: the ways in which people learn. It has come to me that these cultural groupings have compelling power, not simply because of their goals and values, customs, habits, traditions, and so on. Each cultural grouping represents a distinctive way of learning. Youths are drawn to a given cultural grouping because that grouping learns the way they learn. More precisely, they are drawn to a grouping because that grouping learns the way in which they, for the moment, have learned to learn. These cultural groupings have compelling value because they live out and fulfill many of the ways of learning with which God blesses us. Thus, in thinking of the ways in which people learn, I now think of many possibilities.

The multiplicity of ways in which people learn is amazing. You can develop any of these ways of learning. You are not locked into one. You were not born genetically predisposed to only one way. If you have a current propensity for one way, it is simply because you have learned that one way. If you can learn one, you can learn several. The truth is, you can grow any of these ways of learning forward. Select one. Have fun growing it forward. Select another. Have fun growing it forward.

Learning Possibilities

	One-Time	Seasonal	Short-Term (3–5)	Long-Term (6+)	Weekly, Monthly, Year-Round
Athletic, physical					
Intellectual, cognitive					
Extracurricular, work project					
Social, relational					
Fad of the moment					
Over against, outcast					
Independent, individual					
Musical, artistic					
Affective, feeling					
Intuitive, discerning					
Spatial, mathematical					
Meditative, contemplative					
Aesthetic					
Expectant, hopeful					
New ways on the horizon					

This listing of multiple ways of learning is open-ended. There are new ways on the horizon. For this moment, God gives us an extraordinary variety. We have yet to discover all the ways God gives us to learn. Just as our knowledge of the universe is expanding exponentially, so we are discovering and expanding the ways we learn. In the time to come, God will give us new ways to learn that we do not now know. God is generous with grace and with ways of learning.

It is helpful to know that we learn in simultaneous ways, as well as sequentially. Consider a student who is studying a book, listening to the radio, and thinking of a given hope, all at the same time. Or think of the person who is watching two shows on TV, both on the screen at the same time, and reading the newspaper as well. Channel clickers are seeking to do almost simultaneous watching while reading the newspaper.

Consider people who are on a mission team, sharing in a mission project. They are learning simultaneously in a social, relational, and work-project manner. When they sing new songs of the faith as they work, they add the dimension of musical learning.

A strong, healthy congregation encourages all these ways of learning. When it does, it reaches the grass roots. When it does, the level of creativity in people rises amazingly.

Signs of Creativity

I met Sweet Silence and Hilda Mae during a seminar I was leading for about five hundred people. Sweet Silence and her sister, Hilda Mae, had asked to visit with me over lunch one day during the three-day event. We had a remarkable lunch. We laughed and carried on. We shared stories with one another.

Both sisters are short of stature, with gentle eyes, calm faces, and easy dispositions. They live together, helping one another in their early retirement years. Neither has ever married; Hilda Mae came close twice, but for whatever reason, each proposed wedding never happened. I asked them to share with me something about their lives, where they were born, and what had happened since. Each of them shared her life's story.

Sweet Silence began being called by that name because of her plain, sweet personality and because of her quiet, unassuming ways. When I think of Sweet Silence, I think of Francis of Assisi's statement, "Go and preach the Gospel. Use words if necessary." For Sweet Silence, words are hardly ever necessary. In a natural, spontaneous, generous way, she shares the richness of her help with people around her. Sharing just enough help to be helpful—but not so much help that it becomes harmful—she is a wonderful Good Samaritan with her family and friends, and indeed with the whole community.

She is a legend for her hopeful, encouraging spirit and her generous kindness. Her spirit is one of progress, not perfectionism. Gently, graciously, she lives one day at a time. She has solid self-esteem. She is grateful God loves her and thinks well of her. She has a gift for encouraging people, not a drive for power, controlling, and directing. Her life is lived with generous kindness and a gentle, gracious spirit. She is preoccupied neither with wishful thinking nor with an excessive drive toward achievement. She thinks in terms of a few key objectives that are helpful, realistic, and achievable and have solid time horizons. She has a confident sense of hope.

By contrast, Hilda Mae, in her own quiet, persistent manner, learned from somewhere a compulsion toward perfectionism. Somehow, she developed low self-esteem; she thinks more poorly of herself than she has a right to think. These two dynamics together helped her develop a tendency toward power, controlling, and directing. She seems always to be about carefully devising what people should do. In an overcompensating manner, she develops an excessive drive toward achievement. Her tendency is to set too many goals, too high, to be accomplished too soon.

Then she develops a kind of weird, worried, wishful thinking that someone will come and save the day. A few times, this has happened. Someone or some group has come and saved the day for her. Regrettably, this has simply reinforced the intertwining dynamics of perfectionism; low self-esteem; tendency toward power, controlling, and directing; excessive drive toward achievement; and renewed wishful thinking that someone will come and save the day.

Hilda Mae does good works, carefully planned and carried out virtually to perfection. Nothing is ever out of place; everything is in order. She has a tidy spirit about life. Hilda Mae almost never gets upset. She is not mean-spirited. People have never seen her angry or distressed. She seldom weeps. Her spirit feels cautious and constricted. Quiet and determined, she goes about her life and work. People do sense she always attaches some strings to her helping. It is as if she says (without speaking), "I will help you with this. And then I want you to do that." She seeks to control with kindness. She gives gifts with strings.

For Sweet Silence, Life Is	*For Hilda Mae, Life Is*
Progress	Compulsive perfectionism
Solid self-esteem	Low self-esteem
Encouraging spirit	Tendency to power, controlling, directing
Generous kindness	Careful devising
Gentle, gracious spirit	Excessive drive to achieve
Few key objectives, well done	Too many goals, set too high, too soon

Confident sense of hope	Worried, wishful thinking
Natural, spontaneous grace	Cautious, constricted law
Spirit of trust	Spirit of doubt

Creativity and objectives, life and mission—we share them with a spirit of progress, not a compulsion toward perfectionism. A healthy life and a healthy mission—with abundant creativity and solid objectives—have about them a gentle, moving spirit of progress, not a compulsion toward perfectionism.

Progress does not mean that things are always getting better and better, always moving upward and higher. Progress is a matter of living life one day at a time, one step at a time. Progress is learning the art of relaxing, having fun, enjoying life, and living in the grace of God.

Both a spirit of progress and a compulsion toward perfectionism are learned patterns of behavior. The harder of the two to learn is a compulsion toward perfectionism. Compulsive perfectionism goes against the grain of who, and whose, God created us to be. This one requires more energy, drive, and determination because we are working against who God intends us to be. It is easier to learn a spirit of progress. If we can learn the harder one, we can learn the easier one.

Sweet Silence and Hilda Mae are both wonderful women. Again and again, people have taught me that it is easier to have a relationship with Sweet Silence than it is with Hilda Mae. Sweet Silence accepts people for who they are. Hilda Mae does the same, but with her compulsion toward perfectionism she is always trying to get them to be slightly better than who they now are. As a result, the natural, spontaneous, generous basis of the relationship suffers some degree of strain.

It is interesting how Sweet Silence, with a spirit of spontaneous generosity, is helpful with those people around her. Her acts of serving and helping come naturally. There doesn't seem to be much of a plan about them. By contrast, Hilda Mae carefully devises and plans, then delays, delays, and delays. She delays because she wants to be sure she gets it right.

Sometimes, I think this could be the priest and the Levite. It was a messy situation. The man had been beaten and robbed. Not everything could be taken care of neatly and just right. Better to pass by on the other side of the road and find some helping occasion when everything could be done completely and satisfactorily.

When people are around Sweet Silence, they discover their own best creativity. When people are around Hilda Mae, they always have the feeling that her acts of kindness are a way of controlling and directing them toward those ends that she has in mind for them.

Some denominations are like Sweet Silence. They encourage creativity and objectives. They are strong and healthy, flourishing, and having fun. They live a life of progress. They have solid self-esteem and an encouraging spirit. They value generous kindness and a gentle, gracious spirit. They set a few key objectives. They have a confident sense of hope. They live with a natural, spontaneous grace and a spirit of trust.

Some denominations are like Hilda Mae. Regrettably, they learned a compulsion toward perfectionism. They suffer from low self-esteem. They have a tendency to power, controlling, and directing, more than an interest in creativity and objectives. They control with careful kindness. They develop, with polite courtesy and benevolent thoughtfulness, a cautious devising of what the local congregations should do. They teach local congregations that the denomination is there to serve and help local congregations. Then they go on to teach local congregations that the denomination, not the local congregation, knows best how to help.

One denomination, for many years, had an organizational structure that each local church was required to follow. The message was, "We, as the denomination, know best how you, as a congregation, should organize your efforts to share God's mission." Over the years, the denomination revised this structure several times. With each revision, there were hearings, committee meetings, and studies. At the end of each exercise, the denomination sent word to local congregations: "We now know best how you should organize your congregation, so please reorganize yourself in the following way." This denomination continued to decline.

Then, one year, at the national meeting of the denomination, a new possibility emerged. A motion was passed that said a local congregation could organize itself in any way that made best sense to it, with the wisdom and approval of the pastor and the denominational leader for their local area. Time passed. Local congregations began to organize themselves in ways that worked for them. Things seemed to be going well. The new way forward was built on fundamental principles I have encouraged for years:

- We match the plays with the players.
- We send in plays that the players can run, not plays we think the players should run, must run, or ought to run.
- We never send in more plays than the players can run.

Regrettably, the organizational structures in most denominations are designed for the midsize church, not the small, strong congregation and not the large, regional congregation. In *Small, Strong Congregations,* I discuss the four futures available to a congregation:

- Small, strong
- Middle
- Large, regional
- Mega

The two healthiest futures emerging in the twenty-first century, and continuing into the third millennium, are those for the small, strong congregation and the large, regional congregation. Indeed, the vast number of congregations emerging around the world are small, strong congregations.

Yes, there are small, weak congregations, and there are small, dying congregations. Many emerging congregations are small and strong. Middle congregations are like middle colleges; they have virtually gone out of business. In our time, people go to two kinds of college: a small, strong college or a large, regional university. Middle colleges disappeared thirty or forty years ago. Yet some denominations persist in asking the local congregation to organize itself along the structural, institutional ways that worked in middle congregations thirty, forty, and fifty years ago.

The new policy had an encouraging spirit. A local congregation could organize itself in a way that worked for it, with the wisdom of the pastor and the local denominational leader. Healthy, effective congregations began to emerge. Mission and service moved forward. The future began to look promising for many congregations. Regrettably, there are some people in the denomination who are like Hilda Mae: they know what is best. At a later national gathering, in an amendment to another matter, the motion was passed that each congregation must go back to organizing itself according to the organizational structure that the denomination insisted all congregations have.

A healthy denomination trusts the people it ordains, the leaders it elects, and the local congregations it is. A healthy congregation trusts people to have creativity and solid objectives that advance God's mission. A healthy denomination knows the principle of matching the plays with the players. It encourages each local congregation to organize itself wisely, in whatever way works well for it to advance God's mission.

Trust breeds trust. We trust the grace of God. We trust one another. Doubt breeds doubt. We doubt the grace of God. We doubt one another. People live forward or downward to our expectations of them. Yes, when we trust one another, we are on occasion disappointed. I am wise in my trust, not foolish. When someone continues to teach me he or she is not trustworthy, I learn from what he or she is teaching me. I will not be naïve and foolish. I would rather trust and occasionally be disappointed than to doubt and never be disappointed. When we doubt one another, we doubt the grace of God. When we trust one another, we live in the grace of God.

A modest range of traditions and rules, policies and procedures is useful insofar as they help people discover boundaries of love, trust, respect, and confidence with one another. We benefit from some guidelines that help us live well together with each other. However, all the rules and regulations in the galaxies cannot force someone to do something a certain way. Until the person internalizes his or her own sense of creativity and objectives, those rules and regulations amount to so much straw blowing in the wind.

If you trust them, ordain them. If you cannot trust them, do not ordain them. When you ordain them, trust them. If they fail your trust, give them several chances to learn and grow; then help them to an area of work that better matches their best gifts.

When they fulfill your trust, praise them. Ninety out of one hundred fulfill your trust. Encourage them. Help them advance their creativity. Why penalize the ninety—why stifle the creativity of the ninety—to contain the ten? Even as you put containment policies in place, you know they will not contain the ten anyway. The ten ignore them. The ninety follow them, but in following them you stifle their best creativity. The ninety lose. You lose. The congregations lose. The denominations lose. All that loss to contain ten who are not contained anyway. What a waste.

Healthy congregations and denominations encourage the ninety out of one hundred who fulfill the trust placed in them. We have more encouragement policies than containment policies. We help the ninety to build their creativity. We share appreciation, positive recognition, and thank-you. We invest our time in helping them grow. We do not penalize them. We do stifle the creativity of the ninety to contain the ten. Helping people discover their own creativity and objectives is more promising than trying to control and direct what they should do. Controlling and directing congregations, leaders, and pastors may have been promising in some earlier time. Creativity and objectives are more promising in our time.

Recently, I was visiting with the primary leader of a denomination. He is a wonderful friend. We share much together. We have worked well with one another over many years. This denomination has a spirit of grace. It also has a book of rules and regulations. In the book, there is a specified way in which local congregations should organize themselves.

We were having fun visiting that day about creativity and local congregations. I said to my good friend, "Let's think of twenty congregations in the whole denomination that organize themselves exactly the way described in the rules and regulations." I went on to say, "I've had the privilege of visiting, across the land, with many of your local congregations. My sense is they see that section of the rules and regulations as a resource, a guide, a help. With the resources of that section, each congregation has gone on to organize itself in a way that matches its leaders and congregation, and the mission it seeks to live out in the grace of God."

We talked long and late. We had great fun. To our mutual delight, we, together, could not come up with twenty congregations that precisely follow the organizational structure outlined in the rules and regulations. In this denomination, the spirit is grace, not law. The spirit is to encourage the creativity and objectives of local congregations in ways that work well for them. The spirit is not to be insistent on controlling and directing how local congregations must organize themselves.

My friend's denomination does have a spirit of progress, a sense of solid self-esteem, and an encouraging spirit with local congregations. The denomination is gifted with generous kindness, a gentle and gracious spirit, and a few key objectives well done. It shares a confident sense of hope, natural and spontaneous grace, and a spirit of trust in the grace of God and in one another. The signs of creativity are in the life of Sweet Silence. The signs of creativity are in my friend's denomination.

Creativity and Value

Creativity and value are good friends. People want to participate in something that is creative and has value. They long to be creative, not to be directed and controlled. They look forward to being part of a grouping that invites their creative spirit, their excellent ideas, and their good suggestions. They yearn to discover their own creative objectives and strengths rather than being nicely, benevolently told what they should do. People come alive as they share their spirit of creativity. They treasure leaders who trust their wisdom and judgment, their vision and common sense. A healthy congregation cherishes creativity.

A healthy congregation cherishes value. It is helpful to be creative. It is more helpful to be creative in a way that has value—which serves people, families, and communities. People want to focus on something that has worth, that is not incidental and inconsequential. They tire quickly of groups that spend and waste time as though we had a million years.

They look forward to being part of a group that has discovered a few creative ideas that have worthwhile value.

A healthy congregation focuses on projects that count. It does not fritter away resources on possibilities that have fleeting, momentary value. Its members do not allow themselves to be caught up in now this fad, now that fad. They do not rush, now here, now there, trying to do everything. They do not try to do too much too soon. They do not have a ninety-seven-page long-range plan. They know such plans have simply gathered almost everything everyone could think of for possible, tentative conjecture and consideration. By contrast, they have discovered the few creative possibilities with genuine value.

An effective congregation gives opportunities that encourage people's creativity, stir their imaginations, and invite their excellent ideas and good suggestions. Sometimes, we have an open planning retreat, yearly or more often. Frequently, we use the *Twelve Keys to an Effective Church* planning workbook. It is an open gathering. Everyone is invited. Members. Constituents. People served in mission. Friends of the congregation who live elsewhere. Community people.

The retreat feels like a family reunion, a wedding feast of God's grace, a great banquet of God's hope. We share. We pray. We sing. We have fun. We look at the twelve keys to an effective church. We discover our team partner. Our team partner is whoever looks reasonably friendly, sort of half smiling, an intriguing, interesting person. Together, the two of us come up with one idea that is creative and has value. We find another team. We listen to their creative idea. We share ours. Now, the two teams decide the one creative idea they want to share with the whole group. Frequently, the one idea from each team stirs yet a new, third idea that has richer creativity and value.

When the gathered group is large, the two teams, together, select two other teams. They listen to one another. Then, as well as good friends can, they discover the one creative idea that, together as four teams, they want to share with the whole group.

Now, the whole group listens to the ideas coming from the teams and discovers which creative possibilities they will have fun doing this year and the next. On some things, we look three to five years ahead. On some, we look as best one can ten to thirty years ahead. We do not try, this year, to do all of the ideas that emerge. We save some creative ideas for the future.

Some people worry about an open planning retreat. They are concerned that Old So and So will show up and give his tired, worn speech yet another time. We have virtually memorized his speech; we know it by heart. In the process I have suggested, he may get to give his speech to his team partner, and to yet another team. If his idea cannot make it past the round with the team partner he selects, or past the team they select, it does not come to the whole group. If it does come to the whole group, it comes in a form that the others on the two teams have advanced and improved. You will find a full discussion of this process in *Twelve Keys to an Effective Church: The Leaders' Guide*.

Sometimes, the opportunity for creativity is a town-hall meeting of the congregation. Frequently, we use the same process I have just described. Sometimes, grassroots leaders meet with smaller groupings. The expressed purpose is to seek out creative ideas. Sometimes the opportunity is a fellowship gathering of the congregation. Sometimes the opportunity is in the spirit of the leaders: we are open, accessible persons. Our spirit is one of loving, listening, learning, and then leading. We trust one another to be creative in ways that advance the whole. We value, look forward to, count on, and want creative possibilities. We trust the creativity of the whole

Body of Christ. We trust the creativity of God.

We discover the few creative possibilities that have value for our mission. We use five guidelines. In a sense, we test each idea against these guidelines for creativity and value:

- This objective is a creative, decisive possibility. It will make a substantial difference. Twenty percent of the things a group does deliver 80 percent of their results, accomplishments, and achievements. Eighty percent of the things a group does deliver 20 percent of their results, accomplishments, and achievements.
- We will have fun achieving this objective. This objective stirs us as the people of wonder and joy, as the Christmas people. It stirs us as the people of love and compassion, as the people of the Cross. This objective stirs us as the people of new life and hope, as the Easter people.
- This possibility builds on our strengths. It builds on what we do best. It does not build on strengths we wish we had, or on strengths we think we should have. It builds on the strengths God gives us now.
- This objective has value in the world. Directly, this possibility contributes to advancing the character and quality of life on the planet. It strengthens people, families, and groups to live whole, healthy lives in the grace of God. (Note: it does not say, "has value inside the church.")
- This possibility shows promise in serving and advancing God's mission. We are grateful God gives us the gift of mission, as we head into the third millennium.

Frequently, I say to pastors, "Share with me what you have fun doing." For many pastors, this is a puzzling, new invitation. They pause. They stop. They think. A slow, bashful smile begins to appear on their face, like the promise of a rising sun on a clear spring day. It dawns on them that they may never have been asked this question. We discuss what they have fun doing. Then, drawing on Paul's words, I say to them, "God loves a cheerful minister. Do not be a minister out of duty or obligation."

I go on to encourage them: "Share your mission with the generosity and grace of God. Think of what you genuinely, richly, and fully have fun doing. What we have fun doing is God's way of teaching us our strengths. Let your mission be like a wedding feast, a great banquet. Live out what you have fun doing. You will live out the mission with which God blesses you."

You may decide, for example, that you would have fun sharing a mission with children and their families. I have had the privilege of helping many congregations develop such a mission. There are many creative possibilities for mission with children and their families:

Vacation Bible school	Seasonal
Music school	One-time or seasonal
Recreation clinic	One-time or seasonal
Arts and drama clinic	One-time or seasonal
Shepherding visits	One-time or seasonal
School out day	One-time or seasonal
Children's choirs	One-time or seasonal
Special events	One-time or seasonal
Camping	One-time or seasonal
Bible study	One-time or seasonal
Discovery trips	One-time
Mission project	One-time, for children and their families
Summer program	Seasonal

Basketball, baseball, soccer leagues	Seasonal
Children's choirs	Seasonal choirs, fall and/or spring
Children's choirs	Weekly
After school	Weekly
Weekday school	Weekly, for preschool children, etc.
Sunday school	Weekly
Worship	Weekly, for the whole family

School out day is a one-day vacation Bible school on the day of a public school teachers' workday.

Some children's choirs rehearse two or three times and then sing on Christmas, Easter, or on another Special Sunday. Some children's choirs rehearse and sing during the fall semester. Then there is a new opportunity for the spring semester. Some children do the fall semester choir, some the spring semester choir, and some do both choirs. A weekly children's choir starts in September and finishes in May. The only way one can sign up is to plan to be in the choir for the whole school year.

Special events build on the interests of the children and their families.

Trust your creativity. You will discover more possibilities. Try not to do what someone else is doing, just because they are doing it and it is working for them. The art is to select the few that match, for you, the five guidelines for creativity and value.

There are many ways to win a ball game, or to build a house. There are many distinct ways to play or sing a piece of music. There are a vast number of ways to paint a picture of a mountain or build a birdhouse. There are many ways to plant a garden or make a wonderful quilt. The art of creativity is to draw on your imagination and ingenuity. Discover what works for you and has value in sharing the grace and mission of God. I have this confidence: we discover our best creativity when we know that what we are doing has value.

Specific and Concrete

People want to participate in something that is specific and concrete. Given two choices, a generalized mission statement or a blueprint for a building, we build the building. This is not because we are drawn to build buildings. It is because we want to do something specific and concrete. Given a blueprint for mission—a creative plan to serve two hundred children, a plan that is specific and concrete, where we know the objectives we plan to accomplish in years one, two, and three—we do the mission with children. Why? Because it is specific and concrete.

A strong, healthy congregation shares its mission with a specific, concrete spirit, not in a vague or amorphous manner. The members think and live with a focus on key objectives that are specific and concrete. They know the criteria for a key objective. They ask these criteria questions when considering a possible objective:

• Does this objective stir our creativity and imagination, our passion and compassion, our deepest longings and yearnings, our fullest hopes?

• Is it realistic and achievable? Does this objective invite our growth, stretch our strengths and resources? Is it something we can, with the grace of God, accomplish?

• Does it have a solid time horizon? Do we know the date by which we count on achieving the objective? Can we see the steps and time lines backward from that date that lead us forward? (The art of planning is to set the date for the wedding and work backward from that date. People who set the date for their wedding tend to get married.)

• Is it specific and concrete? Have we stated the objective in such a way that we know when we have achieved it? Do we have some measurable sense of what the outcome(s) of the objective look like? (Any statement that includes the word *more* is not an objective. We can never achieve more. More is always one more over the horizon. It is a never-ending horizon of failure.)

• Is it clear as to who will do what, by when, and how? Does the objective give generous authority, rich accountability, and team evaluation?

• Does it match our other key objectives? Taken together, does our set of objectives head us in the same direction, in a complementary, mutually reinforcing spirit?

• Does the objective have the possibility of constructive spillover impact? Could the objective create additional, healthy, productive though originally unplanned benefits? Will we discover new results and outcomes not previously thought of?

• Does the objective lead us to new possibilities of serving God's mission?

I help many congregations that want to be in mission with children and their families. Some of them teach me their objective is to "reach more children." "We need more children" is not an objective. This is an objective: "We look forward to serving two hundred children in the coming three years." We will have some overlaps and returnees. We plan to touch the lives of two hundred distinct children and serve them in the spirit of the grace of God. We look at the possibilities for being in mission with children and their families. We select five objectives we will have fun doing. We could select one. We could select two or three. We select the ones that match us and the children we seek to serve.

Through a seasonal vacation Bible school and through

Objectives for Our Local Congregation

	Number of Children Served		
	Year 1	Year 2	Year 3
Seasonal vacation Bible school	50	65	90
One-time music project	30	40	55
One-time recreation project	70	80	95
One-time mission project	20	35	50
One-time shepherding visits	40	50	70

one-time music, recreation, mission projects, and shepherding visits, we will serve 200 distinct children in the coming three years. The total number of children contacts over the three years adds up to 840. Some children will be part of more than one event. We will serve 200 children.

In the beginning, we identity about fifty to one hundred children we want to serve. We think of their interests. We visit with some of them. We may have a one-time gathering of children and their parents. We discover that some have an interest in vacation Bible school. Some have an interest in music, some in recreation, some in mission. We sense the value of shepherding visits.

We match the plays with the players. We think of the leaders and volunteers who would have fun sharing in this mission. We look for leaders and volunteers from among our members, constituents, people served in mission, community people, and the parents and grandparents of the children we seek to serve. We consider our staffing resources. We develop a blueprint for our mission.

We build our blueprint for our mission with children with

one-time events and a seasonal vacation Bible school. The initial fifty to one hundred children will bring their friends. Their friends will bring their friends. We will serve two hundred children and their families in the course of three years.

We look three years ahead. If we can look three years ahead to build a building (and we do), then we can look three years ahead to build a mission with children. Sometimes we look three months ahead, six months ahead, or a year ahead. In some instances, we look five years ahead. We develop whatever time line makes sense with a specific local congregation.

Let us say we are looking three years ahead. Near the end of the first year, we do these two things. First, we advance the plan for the second and third years. We adjust some things. We delete some things. We modify some things. We add some things. In effect, we create a new first year and a new second year.

The second thing we do is to add the new third year. We have a dynamic, developing three-year mission plan. We have the ability to make improvements and course corrections along the way. We learn from our first year and we look toward ways to advance and improve our mission with children. As the friends of our originating children come on board, we will discover new ideas and new interests that they have. We will grow and develop together.

Our one-time music projects, for each of the three years, will have their own one-time integrity and value. One project may be choral and vocal in nature. One project, the next year, is instrumental in nature. One project combines both. We do not simply repeat the same music project each year just because we did it the previous year.

Likewise, the one-time recreational project in the fall semester is distinct, has its own identity, and focuses on serving and helping particular children in the community. The one-time recreational project for the spring semester or the summer is distinct and has its own identity. We do not automatically repeat each project each year. Similarly, our mission project has its own integrity and identity each year.

We draw on our best creativity. We are not simply repeating, with a pattern of reiteration and redundancy, in the second and third years what we did in the first year. We are drawing on our imagination and innovation to share, with a one-time spirit, the new events and new projects each year. Our creativity is our consistency.

In our example, vacation Bible school has a seasonal focus, with newness each year. In some congregations, vacation Bible school happens year after year after year, and there is a kind of sameness to what is done each year. Here, in this example, year one may focus primarily on athletic-physical and extracurricular–work-project ways of learning. In year two, vacation Bible school focuses on intellectual-cognitive and social-relational ways of learning. In year three, vacation Bible school focuses on musical, affective-feeling, and intuitive-discerning ways of learning.

I am not suggesting this as the normal progression that should happen over a three-year period. I am simply noting that vacation Bible school, year after year in many congregations, is primarily focused on intellectual-cognitive and extracurricular–work project ways of learning. In fact, we can be more creative in helping children learn new ways of learning through the one-time nature, each year, of vacation Bible school.

You will notice the fifth objective is a shepherding visit. The focus is coming to know our children and our families. These are not organizational, institutional visits. We are not trying to get them to do something in the church. These are not recruiting visits. These are people-centered, relational visits. The spirit of the visit is sharing and caring. We are not trying to get them to be more active in the church. We are seeking to be more active in their lives. The visit is effective when it helps them with their lives. The visit is a gift—a sacramental gift of grace, compassion, community, and hope. My book *Visiting in an Age of Mission* will help you with the focus and content of shepherding visits.

Be at peace about the objectives and the numbers in our example. They match well the congregation that has lived them out. They discovered new ideas along the way. They served slightly more than two hundred children over the three years. They continue to discover new possibilities for mission.

In the beginning, they shared their blueprint for mission with the congregation and the community. They invited people to make three-year pledges for the staffing, resources, and scholarships to do the mission. People made generous pledges. As the mission moved forward, giving to the annual budget increased as well. The spirit of the congregation became "We are generous with our mission; we are generous with our giving."

A healthy, effective congregation encourages creativity and objectives. We do not try to control and direct. We do not tell people what they should or must do. We help people advance their ways of learning. We develop the signs of creativity. We focus on objectives that are creative and have value. We encourage people to accomplish objectives they have decided to pursue and for which they have ownership. We develop a blueprint for mission with a few specific, concrete objectives that match the criteria for a key objective.

We are grateful for the creativity of God. Our creativity comes from God's creativity. It is God's gift. We create because God creates. We create because God gives us the gift of creativity. We discover our creativity and our objectives. We live creative, healthy lives in the grace of God.

7

A Focus on the Whole of Life

O give thanks to the Lord, for he is good; for his steadfast love endures forever!

PSALMS 106:1

There is a time to focus on the whole of life. There is a time to focus on the parts. This is a time to focus on the whole. One possibility for reaching and growing the grass roots is to encourage people to discover and live the whole of life, not just part of life, not just an inside-the-church life. God lives in the whole of our lives. God's grace touches the whole of our lives. God invites us to live whole lives:

- As persons
- As congregations
- As leaders
- In our serving

As Persons

God encourages us to enjoy and celebrate the whole of life.

Late in the year,
on a crisp autumn morn
I'm loading my boat,
on a bank that is worn.

The river is calling,
to those who will listen
Come ride my waters,
soft currents that glisten.

I toss in my gear
And push off from the shore
Banks that once echoed
from native folklore.

Clear crystal waters,
I long to behold
Dancing with fish,
shimmering of gold.

With each careful stroke,
on this river I lust
The leaves softly whisper,
as they turn into rust.

A canvas of colors
has alerted my senses
To cows quietly grazing,
behind wooden fences.

I lean with my shoulder,
my paddle must bend
as I answer the river,
for I am her friend.

My cares wash away,
in all of her treasures
She's one of God's gifts,
my mind cannot measure.

The wind at my back,
I'm gracefully gliding
So grateful to be,
Red River Riding.

Our son, Mike, wrote this poem during a canoeing trip on the Red River. The poem is a wonderful celebration of the whole of life. He calls it *Red River Riding*. He did the trip and wrote the poem to celebrate a succession of remarkable events in his life. In appreciation for our help, he was generous in sharing the poem with Julie and me. We all experience amazing events and remarkable discoveries in our lives. We celebrate the whole of life.

Christ came to give us abundant life. He did not come just to the "religious part" of our life. He came to the whole of our life. He did not come to give us an inside-the-church life. The purpose of church is to help people live the whole of life in the whole of the universe in the light of the whole Gospel. The purpose of church is not to become the whole of life.

The whole is more than just a collection of parts. The whole of life includes:

- Family
- Vocation
- Education
- Civic and community
- Business
- Hobbies, interests
- Political
- Recreational
- Aesthetic, music, arts
- Relational, social
- Health
- Religion

We discover the whole of the Gospel for the whole of life. In doing so, we live whole lives in the grace of God.

God encourages us to have a sense of harmony in our lives. The art of living a healthy life is integration, not fragmentation. The music of our lives does consist of many tempos, chord compositions, and major and minor keys; it is played in various places on different instruments and in concert with many other musicians. The beauty of music is the integration of many parts—dissonance evolving to harmony, with numerous notes involved, the magic of a theme and variations on it, counterpoint seeming to go in all directions only to come together in a wonderful unity. Finally, for both listeners and players, the beauty of the music is the sense of coherence, completion, and satisfaction in the experience of the whole.

Think of a musical composition. It is made up of a multitude of distinct measures. Each measure is, in some ways, set apart. Yet, one measure entirely detached from all the other measures is meaningless. One could separate all the measures on many pages, simply leaving them printed under the same name, and on the same size page as before they were separated. This would not make an integrated, easily moving, flowing composition. With music of any kind, the measures connect and flow, one into the next. There is an overall wholeness, a compelling whole carried out in innumerable tiny measures of music. The parts, by themselves, do not make music. The whole helps us sing.

The beauty of a quilt is the integration of many parts. Pieces and blocks, scattered around the quilt room. Each, in itself, with a special beauty. Thread and needles. Fabrics. All kinds. Sewing machine and cutting board. Batting. More fabrics. Patterns and pictures. Value and colors. They are gathered in the same room. They do not make a quilt. They are a collection of the parts. The art of quilt making is to create a whole out of the parts. When we look at the finished quilt, our eyes see the whole, the wonder and beauty of a work of art. For both quilters and family, the beauty of the quilt is the sense of harmony and unity, coherence and integration of the quilt. We experience the whole.

Paint does not make a picture. We can have blue, red, and yellow paints and all the variations thereof. We can have pens, frame, canvas, and brushes. We can have a person. An easel. A color palette. They can be in the same room. They do not make a picture. When the picture is finished, it is more than a collection of parts. It has a sense of beauty, of wonder, of joy about it. It is a whole.

A court. A net at each end. A coach. A basketball. Five people. Separately, they do not make a team. The swift-moving flow of a fast break happens because the five have become a team, a whole. They are not ball hogs. They are not preoccupied with their own territory, status, or position. As they move down the court, they move as one. They know where each other will be, virtually without looking. A sense of harmony. A spirit of unity. They are together. They are a whole.

In medicine, now, we focus on the sources of health. We used to focus primarily on illnesses. Sometimes, we did so by concentrating on this illness or that illness, as distinct and separate. We are wiser now. Our research is more advanced. Even in some ancient traditions of healing, people had insight into the wholeness of health. We understand, more fully, the integrative nature of our physical, emotional, thinking, and spiritual well-being. We have come to understand "You can't have one without the other." Things go together.

The art of living a whole, healthy life is integration, not fragmentation. The art is developing a life lived as a whole, not a life lived in separate compartments and departments.

God invites us to live life with a spirit of unity and a sense of coherence. God encourages us to have a sense of harmony about our living.

We could live life in separate compartments. Rushing here and there, out of our vocation compartment into our recreation department. Slam that door and on to our civic and community compartment, and from there to our family department. Rushing here and there. Slam that door and on to our religious compartment. We would have made this the ghetto where God lives. Slam that door and on to the business compartment. On and on, back and forth.

We could develop differing selves for each part of life, fragmenting and fracturing life into pieces, keeping each compartment separate and distinct. We would invest considerable time, energy, and effort in doing so. We might bring it off— keeping life a collection of separate parts. What would we gain? We would gain a life of confusion and fragmentation, frustration and failure. We would be preoccupied with the measures and never hear the music. We would live a life of dissonance and distraction, never fully developing the strengths God gives us. We would be running against the grain of who God creates us to be.

The whole Gospel is for the whole of your life. Jesus describes the Kingdom of God as a wedding feast, a great banquet. Life is to be like a wedding feast of God's grace, a great banquet of God's hope. There are trials and tribulations, difficulties and disappointments, failures and defeats, anxiety and anger, fear and dread. We live through all of these best, though, when we live life as a whole, discovering the grace and hope of God.

Twelve Keys for Living encourages people to live life as a whole. The book invites you to look at twelve possibilities that contribute to a whole, healthy life. It encourages you to discover your strengths, gifts, and competencies among the twelve, and in a holistic, integrative spirit grow and develop, advance and build the life with which God blesses you.

Twelve Keys for Living

Mission	Joy
Compassion	Wisdom
Hope	Encouragement
Community	Creativity
Leadership	Health
Simplicity	Generosity

The genius, the helpfulness, of the twelve keys for living is that they invite us:

- To look at the whole of life
- To claim the whole of life, and the strengths with which God blesses us
- To expand the whole of life, to build on our strengths
- To add new strengths that advance the whole of life
- To think, act, and live the whole of life

God invites us to a life of unity and harmony, coherence and integration. God does not want us to live in separation and dissonance, fragmentation and compartmentalization. God encourages us to live the whole Gospel in the whole of our lives.

As Congregations

Effective, healthy congregations live the whole of life. Congregations that live as a collection of parts influence people to live as a collection of parts. A departmental congregation creates departmental people. The art is integration. The art is developing a congregation that lives life together as the Body of Christ, as a whole.

A weak, declining, or dying congregation lives life in separate compartments. It keeps each compartment distinct and disconnected. Its members invest considerable time, energy, and effort in doing so. They run against the grain of who God creates them to be. They think and live not as the Body of Christ but as a collection of separate bones, joints, and muscles. Now and then, they almost bring it off. In the end, they become weaker. They decline. They die.

In *Twelve Keys to an Effective Church,* I discuss the qualities, the possibilities that contribute to a holistic, effective congregation.

Twelve Keys for a Strong, Healthy Congregation

Mission objectives	Competent programs
Visitation, shepherding	Open accessibility
Dynamic worship	High visibility
Relational groupings	Land, parking
Solid leadership	Space, facilities
Decision making	Generosity, finances

The genius of the twelve keys for a strong, healthy congregation is that they invite a congregation of people to look at the whole of their life together. It encourages them to see the interrelationship of the twelve qualities that contribute to a healthy life. The focus is on an integrated understanding of what it means to be a strong, healthy congregation.

In worship, an effective congregation shares a service that has about it a spirit of the whole. The opening music by the organist, the choral introit by the choir, the invocation by the pastor, and the opening hymn shared by the congregation build on one another. There is a dynamic, a commonality of texture and spirit shared by these four events as they begin a service of worship.

Recently, I was in one of our major congregations. The organist played the opening music, the choir sang the introit, the pastor gave the invocation, and the opening hymn was sung by the congregation. Each in itself was well done, but the only thing they had in common was that they happened one after another on a Sunday morning in approximately the same location in the galaxies. None of these events had any connection with any other. I do not mean in terms of the content of the words. They had no sense of texture and spirit, harmony and unity. They were like four separate measures. They did not make a piece of music. They were like four excellent quilt blocks. Together, they did not make a quilt. They had no quality of building the service of worship, of drawing us closer to the grace of God.

In a healthy service of worship, there is a sense of the whole. The music, the liturgy, and the preaching are not alternating, separate, distinct tracks. I find myself in some services like that. The music is one track. The liturgy is one track. The preaching is one track. They happen, one after another, alternating back and forth, on a Sunday morning. The music leader and the pastor work hard to be sure the words of the music match the message of the morning, to fit the theme of that service, but a whole service is more than a common theme. In a whole service, the spirit of the music, the spirit of the liturgy, and the spirit of the message match. They create an interweaving dynamic, a harmony, a unity. Together, music, liturgy, and message contribute to the whole of our worship of God. You will find my book *Dynamic Worship* a helpful resource.

In a healthy congregation, the children's choirs and the children's Sunday school are good friends. The children's choir directors and their Sunday school teachers are good friends. They share with one another. The themes match. Each semester, and sometimes each week, the themes studied in Sunday school and the themes of the songs the children are learning in their choirs strengthen one another. They rein-force one another, helping children to discover—both in the teaching and in the music—the whole of the Gospel they are learning. Frequently, the Sunday school classes, the children's choirs, and the worship services have matching themes, learnings, and dynamics.

In a weak, declining, or dying congregation, what hap-pens in Sunday school and what happens in children's choirs during the week have no connection to one another. The teachers and the choir directors do not communicate with one another. They do not reinforce one another. It is as if they were on different planets from one another, or even in differ-ent galaxies.

In an effective, healthy congregation, the youth program is for youths and their families. The leaders of the youth pro-gram know that what they are about is advancing the quality of life with the young people and their families. In a weak, declining, or dying congregation, there is a separate division for children, a separate division for youths, and a separate division for adults. The youth program is for the young peo-ple only. Regrettably, pied pipers lead those separate youth programs. They say to the youths, "Come off with me on this retreat, and we will talk long and late into the night, and I will teach you what life is really all about. Your parents are old fuddy-duddies, and they do not know."

Kids and parents have enough difficulty relating to one another during the teenage years, without the mixed blessing of the disjunctive, divisive separatism of a pied piper. Indeed, these days in a congregation when we hire the youth director, we do not hire a youth director. We bring onto the team someone whose focus is as director with youths and their families. We serve the whole family with the whole program.

A strong, healthy congregation has a wonderful spirit of welcoming new people into the family. The spirit is a generous, inviting welcome, whether it is a small, strong; a healthy mid-size; a large, regional; or a megacongregation. The spirit is, "Glad you are part of the family." Both reaching and growing the grass roots are good friends. Healthy congregations know this. We live out this wholeness, this consistency as we welcome new members. We reach them with a focus on the whole of life. We help them grow with a focus on the whole of life.

We are consistent. We grow the grass roots the same way we reach them. We reach the grass roots one way. We help them to grow the same way.

A Strong, Healthy Congregation Reaches and Helps People with These Qualities

Movement

Compassion

Living in God's universe

Excellent sprinter culture

Grassroots mission

Creativity and objectives

Focus on the whole of life

We welcome new members as part of the family, not as members of an organization. The new-member orientation meeting is really a "welcome to the family" get-together. We share with one another something of ourselves, where we were born, what has happened since, and what we have fun doing. The new member gathering is more like a shower before a wedding than a business orientation. It is more like a family reunion than an introduction to all of the programs and activities of the church and how one can volunteer. The gathering is people-centered and relational; not organization-centered, institution-centered, and functional.

During the gathering, we encourage new members to look forward to the fun of sharing in:

- A one-time mission project. We learn a theology of serving as we participate in a mission project.

- A one-time *Twelve Keys for Living* seminar. We discover the qualities of a whole, healthy life, and learn the ways we can grow them forward in our own lives. We learn our strengths, gifts, and competencies to advance our whole life.

- A one-time Bible study. We have the opportunity to discover the meanings of a given, specific passage of scripture. In doing so, we discover ways of studying the Bible and help to advance our understanding of the Christian life.

- A one-time prayer and worship experience. We discover possibilities for growing our life of prayer and worship.

- A one-time shepherding experience. We have the privilege of visiting with some person or group, where we share a simple gesture of grace, compassion, community, and hope.

We have this confidence about new members. They can grow themselves. We cannot grow them. We can share suggestions and possibilities. We can share encouragement and assurance. We can share our own wisdom and experience. Finally, each person grows himself or herself. No one else can do that for the individual.

We share with new members all five possibilities. We invite, we encourage them to select whichever three of the five they know will help them grow their life forward. The focus is not on what they can do for us. The focus is not on what we can do with them. The focus is on what they can do for themselves to grow forward a whole, healthy life in the grace of God.

In an earlier time, a time of institutions, we could reach the grass roots in an institutional way, and we could help them to grow in an institutional way.

Congregations in an Institutional Time Reach People and Help Them Grow with These Qualities

Institution

Commitment

Solid marathon culture

Top-down mission

Controlling and directing

Focus on inside-the-church life

Reaching and growing the grass roots in this manner worked because it was a time of institutions. Regrettably, we continue to remember when that approach worked.

Some congregations almost understand the new time in which we live. Now, they try to reach the grass roots with a focus on the whole of life. However, when they try to help the grass roots grow, they fall back into an old institutional pattern. We can no longer reach the grass roots one way and then try to grow them another way. We can no longer reach them in a movement way and then try to grow them in an institutional way.

A weak, declining, or dying congregation is inconsistent. It reaches the grass roots one way. Then it tries to help them grow another way. They do a bait-and-switch. New-member orientations are a bait-and-switch from movement to institution, family to organization, community to committee, and the whole of life to part of life. The catch is that this bait-and-switch no longer works (if it ever did).

A Weak, Declining, or Dying Congregation

Tries to Reach People with These Qualities	But then, It Tries to Help Them Grow with These Qualities
Movement	Institution
Compassion	Commitment
Living in God's universe	Ignoring discoveries of God's universe
Excellent sprinter culture	Solid marathon culture
Grassroots mission	Top-down mission
Creativity and objectives	Controlling and directing
Focus on the whole of life	Focus on inside-the-church life

The bait is the movement, the compassion, the making sense of life in God's universe, the excellent sprinter possibilities, the grassroots mission, the creativity and objectives, and the focus on the whole of life. These qualities draw people to become new members.

The switch is to the institution, the commitment, the planet without the stars, the solid marathon runner possibilities, the top-down maintenance, the control and directing, and a focus on the parts. These qualities are not the ones that new members were looking for when they came.

Usually, the attempt at a switch comes at the time of new-member assimilation. The new-member orientation sessions are carefully, thoughtfully planned. Each church committee wants equal time to get its message across to the new members. A parade of opportunities to volunteer to do work inside the church are presented to the new members. The message is polite, quiet, and insistent. The message is:

- We welcome you as new members.

- Now that you are a new member, we want you to decide where you plan to fulfill your commitment.

- The church you joined has needs you can answer (slots you can fill). Look at the new-member "opportunities volunteer list" and select where you would like to volunteer.

When the new members look at the list, they discover mostly a long list of solid marathon runner jobs, the focus of which is inside the church. They begin to discover that the church they thought they had joined does not exist. They are on their way to becoming new inactive members.

You decide to join a group of people who talk about mission and serving. You want to serve and do mission. Will you stay with the group once you discover the group is preoccupied with surviving and maintenance? If you order a certain meal in a restaurant, and the waiter brings you an entirely different meal, will you go back to that restaurant?

What drew the new members was the sense of mission and compassion, but now we show our true colors and teach them we are an institution, with obligation and commitment. We teach them we are not interested in their whole life. Our interest is in their inside-the-church life. They do not immediately become inactive members. They simply begin to decide that what they thought they were joining is not who we really are. They begin, almost without realizing it, to look elsewhere for a grouping where they can fulfill their interest in the whole of life.

People want their lives to count in some tangible, worthwhile way. They join a congregation with expectancy and hope. The bait-and-switch happens. It creates slightly disillusioned people who seek elsewhere a grouping that has an interest in mission. They are not angry at the church. They simply view the institution that has done the bait-and-switch on them with a slightly innocuous spirit, as a pleasant irrelevancy in their life. They recede into the woodwork, become inactive, and seek elsewhere.

Congregations that live as a whole create people who live as a whole. We reach the grass roots in ways in which we actually can reach them, not the ways we think we should reach them. We focus on living life as a whole; thus we create people who live as a whole, not just an inside-the-church life. We encourage people to discover and live the whole of life, in the whole of God's grace.

As Leaders

As healthy leaders, we focus on the whole of life, not just on an inside-the-church life. That would be a "parts" view of life.

One year, Mary Beth and I were discussing the possibility of her leadership in our congregation. The nominating committee and I had invited her to serve as chair of the finance committee. She is a gifted, effective leader. We knew she would do solid work in advancing the finances of our congregation. She asked for time to think about it.

Four days later, we visited. She said to me, "I'm happy to serve as chair of the finance committee. I'm honored to be invited. I know I can help in that post. I can take that post, or I can serve as chair of the new task force to help the poor who live in the slums of our city. I can't do both. I would appreciate your thoughts on the better possibility." Without hesitation, I said, "Mary Beth, let's do the project to help the poor. We'll figure out who can serve as chair of the finance committee."

In that conversation, I discovered how much I was preoccupied with *inside the church*. My focus had been on helping people fulfill their leadership competencies inside the church. I simply thought that way. It did not dawn on me to think any other way. In the conversation with Mary Beth, this new thought came to me. I had not previously thought the matter through. The new idea was just there. It was obvious that Mary Beth could mobilize the resources of the city to help poor families.

As leaders, we develop the qualities that help us focus on the whole of life, not simply inside the church. The next pair of lists help many congregations in encouraging these qualities. The contrast is striking between leaders of the whole and leaders of a part. Congregational leaders who live the whole of life are leaders of strong, healthy congregations. Those who live a part of life are leaders of weak, declining, or dying congregations.

Leaders of the Whole	*Leaders of a Part*
Team	Department
Whole	Part
Three years ahead	One year ahead
Major priorities for the whole	Departmental plans
Key objectives	General goals
Flexible structure	Stiff structure
"How can I help?"	"That's not in my area."
"Let's do this together."	"I'm in charge of that."
"We are a solid team."	"I'm glad to help in my own area."
Accomplishments	Responsibilities
Authority	Duties
Accountability to the team	Top-down evaluation

Healthy leaders create healthy congregations. Together, they think, value, and live the qualities of leadership that contribute to the whole of life. I encourage you to study *Effective Church Leadership* for further resources.

Grassroots leaders reach grassroots people. Grassroots leaders focus on the whole of life. Top-down leaders focus on part of life, namely, the institution of which they are a leader. Be a top-down leader, and you reach top-down people. Be a grassroots leader, and you reach grassroots people. Fortunately, I have the privilege of sharing and working with more and more grassroots leaders. Their number grows.

Note the qualities of grassroots leaders:

- Initial reluctance to lead
- Compelling events stir their compassion
- The grass roots "create" them as a leader
- Identify with the grass roots
- Give themselves away in serving the cause, the mission
- Focus on the whole of life

Top-down leaders are marked by these qualities:

- Eager to lead
- Enjoy the power
- Seniority system helps them work their way up the ladder
- Identify with the institution
- Continue to seek to expand their power, protect the institution, and thereby protect their position and identity
- Focus on an inside-the-church life

Grassroots leaders focus on living life in the world. They focus on the whole of life with all its dimensions: family; vocation; education; civic and community; business; hobbies and interests; political; recreational; aesthetic, music, and arts;

relational and social; health; and religion. Indeed, they do not divide life into separate components. They see the religious dynamic of life as central to all the dimensions of life. They see the whole of life in all of life.

Top-down leaders assume that if one participates in an inside-the-church life, one is therefore living a whole, healthy life. Sometimes they sense there is more to life than being inside the church. On occasion, they assume that living an inside-the-church life prepares one for living a whole, healthy life. Mostly, they focus on only part of life. They are dimly aware of all the dimensions of life.

However, they are preoccupied with their inside-the-church view. They divide life into separate components. They focus on the religious compartment. Their frame of reference is inside the church. They see part of life as the whole of life. Grassroots leaders have this confidence: the whole of life is more than part of life.

One evening, I was speaking to a large gathering of about eight hundred people. Sitting next to me at the speakers' table was a shy, quiet individual, whose wife was next to him. We began a conversation during dinner. I said to him, "Share with me about yourself." With a spirit of gentle humility, he described that at fifteen years of age, he had learned to fly planes. In his country, he found he had a considerable gift for flying. By seventeen, he was flying bombers for his country. Time passed. His country entered a war. Even though he was still quite young, he flew hundreds of missions during the course of the war. The leader of his country decorated him with the Iron Cross. He was a national hero.

He said to me, "Dr. Callahan, I came to know that I was serving in the wrong cause when they became more concerned for the plane than for the pilot. I remember the day I landed the plane after a fierce dogfight in the air, and those in charge were more concerned that the plane got back safely

than that the pilot got back safely. They became more interested in planes than in pilots."

He went on to say, "In the time since that war, I have lived
a wonderful life, contributing as best I can to the welfare of
humanity. I want you to know that my interest is in people. I can
confirm what you are sharing with us about the whole of life."

In another year, in another part of the country, I led a
weekend planning retreat for the whole of the denomination
in that state. During our time together, we moved through
four sharing and planning steps. As step one, I encouraged
each person to find a team partner and to develop one excellent idea or good suggestion that would advance our mission
together as God's people. We were a large group. Therefore,
as step two, I encouraged them to find four other teams and
share their ideas with each other. They were to choose just
one idea (and it might be a totally new idea) that occurred to
all five teams as the best way forward.

When they completed that step, I asked them, as step
three, to find one other group, composed of five teams. Each
group of five teams was to share its one good idea with the
other group of five teams. After listening creatively and considering the two ideas, they were to form one excellent idea
or good suggestion that they were convinced would advance
God's mission. As step four, each group (five teams plus five
teams) shared their one excellent idea with the whole, gathered group.

We did these sharing and planning steps in a good-fun,
good-time spirit, thoughtfully, deliberately, with a mixture of
singing, worshipping, and praying over that weekend. It was
amazing what happened. The grassroots groups discovered
excellent ideas and good suggestions that came to the whole
group for consideration. There were no long speeches given
by the same people who ordinarily spoke year after year,
speeches that we had long ago memorized. Instead, there was

sharing, conversation, creativity, and the discovery of possibilities that advanced the whole. The key objectives, the group decided, were to find ideas that were thoughtful, forward thinking, and well matched with the mission field God gives them.

After it was all over and we had concluded our worship service of celebration, many people spoke with appreciation for the spirit of the sessions and of all that we had accomplished together. As I was about to leave, nine people came to visit with me. They wanted to share with me how upset and angry they were. They did not know who else to talk to, so they wanted to visit with me. I listened thoughtfully, politely, graciously, gently. Finally, after they had shared with me for some time, I said to them, "You seem to be upset for these reasons. One, you did not get to tell the grass roots what they should do, must do, or ought to do. The grassroots people discovered their own best ways forward.

"Two, you seem aggravated because the grassroots people's objectives are more advanced and forward-thinking than any proposals you have presented in recent years. I think you are angry because, when given half a chance, the grassroots people's objectives and their interest in achieving them are ahead of where you are."

I went on to say to the group of nine: "If there is a third reason you are upset, it is because they did not buy your plan. The problem is that you are more interested in your own particular plan than you are in the people. It shows. You are not interested in their ideas. You only want them to agree to yours. You can be at peace about your own plan. The grass roots have moved well beyond your plan. I encourage you to learn to have a genuine interest in the grassroots congregations in this state."

Grassroots leaders are more interested in the people than the plan. They are people-driven, not institution-driven. Grassroots leaders are local-driven, not top-down-driven; strength-driven, not weakness-driven; spirit-driven, not size-driven; compassion-driven, not commitment-driven; community-driven, not challenge-driven; hope-driven, not memory-driven; mission-driven, not maintenance-driven.

The grass roots respond to leaders from their own, because these grassroots leaders have five remarkable advantages in their favor, five major strengths with which they are able to reach the grass roots:

1. Grassroots leaders think, plan, feel, behave, act, dream, and live like the grass roots. They know and under-stand the grass roots, because they *are* the grass roots. They have not lost their sense of being the grass roots themselves.
2. They focus on the whole of life. They help the grass roots with all the dimensions of life.
3. They have a compelling interest in serving the grass roots. They have a deep longing to serve their children, their parents, their grandparents, and their grandchil-dren. They have a longing to serve their families and their clans—and the whole of humanity. They long to serve the vast communities of people who live at the grass roots.
4. They love the grass roots. The grass roots love them. They remember how the grassroots people live. They set aside any personal stake for themselves. They have a deep personal identity with the grass roots. They freely share power and eagerly help the grass roots dis-cover internal sources of power for their lives.
5. They trust the grass roots. Thus the grassroots people trust them. Grassroots leaders have confidence in the creativity and imagination, the wisdom and insight of the grass roots. They actively seek out excellent ideas

and good suggestions from the grass roots. The sense of ownership and trust are mutual. Trust breeds trust.

I am grateful for the increasing number of grassroots leaders in major denominational movements. Their contributions are helpful, healthy, and increasingly having value and impact. We are seeing major advances in a grassroots understanding of leadership.

Top-down leaders do not connect with the grass roots. They may want to. They may yearn to. For all their yearnings and good intentions, top-down leaders cannot reach the grass roots. Even when they want to, they have five noteworthy strikes against them, five major hurdles to overcome:

1. Top-down leaders have been top-down in their thinking, planning, acting, and living for so long that they have forgotten how grassroots people think, plan, feel, dream, act, and live.

2. They focus on the parts. They see life as a collection of parts, and the important part for them is the inside-the-church, institutional part.

3. They have a vested interest in keeping their own top-down institutional bureaucracy going. They frequently rationalize that they can do both. However, one cannot simultaneously ride a disjointed, half-blind, backward-going, whopper-jawed camel and at the same time run a one-hundred-yard dash. Either you stay on the lopsided camel, or you get off and run the race.

4. Even if they could remember how grassroots people think and live, and even if they could set aside their vested interest in the institution, which they love and in which they have immersed their own deep personal identity, they are reluctant to give up the power they have spent years in acquiring. It takes a rare act of true humility to give up that power, step back, and transfer that power to the grass roots.

5. Then there is the matter of trust. Even if they could remember how the grass roots think, feel, and live, and even if they could set aside their vested interest in the institution, which they love, and in which they have immersed their own deep personal identity, and even if they could give up the power they have spent years in acquiring, they still face this dilemma: the grass roots do not trust them. The reason: top-down leaders do not trust the grass roots. Thus the grass roots do not trust them. Mistrust breeds mistrust. Top-down leaders think they know what the grass roots should do. They do not trust them to discover excellent ideas and good suggestions to advance the whole. Institutional leaders feel, in a genuinely benevolent manner, that they know what is best for the grass roots. The grass roots have no ownership for the ideas that top-down leaders seek to impose, "for their own good," on the grass roots. The consequence is that institutional leaders have virtually no mutual grounds of trust, respect, credibility, and confidence with the grass roots. They do not trust the grass roots. The grass roots do not trust them.

Top-down leaders are sincere, decent, and for the most part competent people. They do not get angry or upset. They seldom make mistakes. Indeed, their compulsion toward per-fectionism causes them to look with horror upon mistakes. That is one reason they craft so many policies and procedures, rules and regulations, conditions and stipulations. They are quietly relentless in their two cherished notions: one, the grass roots do not know what is best for them, and two, in their wise benevolence the top-down leaders know what is best for the grass roots. They have a hierarchical view of the world.

Luther is grassroots. Calvin is grassroots. Francis of Assisi is grassroots. Wesley is grassroots. They all learned it from Jesus. Jesus is grassroots.

Some leaders of institutions do a solid job of reaching the grass roots. I enjoy sharing and working with them. We are good friends. We thrive together. They have a spirit of humility, a sense of grace, and a gift of compassion. They trust the grass roots. They are willing to give up a focus on the institution they have loved for so long and instead focus—with the grass roots—on the whole of life. They are remarkable people. Their number is increasing. I see more of them every day. The world has changed, and they are changing. I see fewer and fewer top-down leaders. I see an increasing number of grassroots leaders whose contributions to God's mission are extraordinary.

To thrive, a congregation has to be more than a collection of parts. It has to have some sense of wholeness about it. People are not drawn to congregations, nor to denominations, that are simply a collection of parts, bickering, fussing, and feuding, clamoring to be sure each part gets its share of the pie. People already participate in enough groupings like that— employment, civic, political groupings, where bickering is the order of the day. Why join another group that is bickering?

In Our Serving

We are here to serve in the world. We discover the whole of life in serving. We live beyond ourselves. We discover ourselves. We find life, mission, and power in serving, not in being served.

A long time ago, in a faraway land, the notion was that the local congregations served the denomination, and a clear message went out: "Local congregations are here to serve the denomination." Congregations would gather their resources, both in volunteers and money, and send them to the denomination. The denomination, in its wisdom, would then distribute these volunteer and financial resources all over the planet.

The system worked well for a long, long time. Then, it began to work less well. It became harder and harder to convince local congregations to send their volunteer and financial resources to the denomination. Reluctance and resistance came to visit. In some groupings, the giving increased, but the price was a persistent nagging at congregations. Reluctance and resistance increased. Mission and service giving began to falter; not too much, but enough to worry people in the denominational headquarters.

The idea emerged that the denomination is here to serve the local congregation. I am not certain any one ever said it out loud, but the implication was sent forth: the denomination had it all wrong back then. It is not that local congregations are to serve the denomination. It is that the denomination is here to serve the local congregations.

A number of denominations made a 180 degree turn and began to serve local congregations. Some just said it but never did it. Some did it.

God invites both local congregations and denominations to serve God's mission in the world. God does not invite local congregations to serve the denomination. That is an inside-the-church perspective. Likewise, God does not invite the denomination to serve local congregations. That is an inside-the-church view of life. We already have enough self-serving congregations. We do not need to reinforce that unhealthy pattern any further.

Congregations and denominations do not exist to serve one another. God encourages congregations and denominations to look at the whole of life, to serve God's mission in the world. I am encouraged to see the increasing number of grassroots pastors and leaders who understand this. I am thankful that we share together in this common mission. Increasingly, many people are coming to understand that the text does not say, "For God so loved the local congregation." It does not say, "For God so loved the denomination." The text is profoundly clear, "For God so loved the world." The text helps us understand the mission is in the world, not in the church.

We are here to love and serve the world. We are not here to save denominations. We are not here to save local congregations. The irony is that we might save both, but miss the extraordinary invitation God gives us. We are here to serve the world, not one another.

I do not really know, but the priest in the story of the Good Samaritan may have believed that the local church is supposed to serve the denomination, and so he passed by on the other side of the road. The Levite may have believed that the denomination is supposed to serve local congregations, and so he passed by on the other side of the road. They may even have been on their way to some conference to discuss their views.

The Samaritan, the one least expected to do so, stopped, bound up the wounds of the man, beaten and robbed, and took him to an inn. The Samaritan understood the whole of life is found in serving. A healthy, effective congregation serves the mission of God. As a mission team of leaders, grassroots people, and pastor, we invest our strengths and resources in serving. We discover the whole of life.

The Future That Has Come

Some people decide to live in the future that has come. Some decide to live in the past that has been. Some congregations do the same. God gives us the privilege of choosing. Healthy people and healthy congregations live this way.

- We think, plan, behave, act, and live as a movement, not as an institution.

- We share the motivations of compassion, community, and hope more than challenge, reasonability, and commitment. The first three are our majors; the second three are our minors.

- We encourage people to make sense of life in this universe and on this planet rather than ignore the discoveries of the universe we are making.

- We help people grow with a balance of excellent sprinter and solid marathon runner possibilities rather than a primary focus on solid marathon runner possibilities.

- We encourage people to participate in mission projects that are direct, generous, just enough, and grassroots rather than indirect (remote), conserving, too much (not enough), and top-down.

- We help people discover their best creativity and the development of objectives, for which they have ownership, rather than controlling and directing what they should do.

- We encourage people to discover and live the whole of life, not just an inside-the-church life.

Healthy people and healthy congregations are discovering and living out these major paradigm shifts in their life and mission. The result is that they have the gifts and the abilities to reach and grow the grass roots.

In our time, people need help with these major paradigm shifts. They want to discover how they can deal with, cope with, benefit from, and live out these paradigm shifts in their own lives. They look for a grouping of people, a congregation that is doing so creatively and successfully. They are drawn to this congregation as a source of help and hope. They are not drawn to a congregation that has ignored the future that has come. They are drawn to the group that is doing well what they hope to do well in their own lives—

namely, wrestling with, coming to terms with, discovering, growing, and building on the major paradigm shifts of this new time.

Congregations that build on these paradigm possibilities become strong, healthy, and effective. They contribute much to God's mission. They are healthy because of their strengths and spirit, not their size. Many are small, strong congregations. Many are large, regional congregations. They have a theology of serving, a theology of mission. They are developing these paradigm shifts in their thinking, planning, feeling, dreaming, acting, and living. They are strong. They are healthy. They live with the future that has come.

Some people decide to live in the past that has been. Some congregations do the same. They decide to be part of the past that has been rather than the future that has come. They decide not to discover, benefit from, and live out the paradigm shifts with which God has blessed us.

Weak, declining congregations are tentative about the future that has come. They may discover and live out one or two of the paradigm shifts. They almost think about the possibility of considering that maybe they could, somehow, sometime, contemplate moving toward the potentiality of living out some of the paradigm shifts. They draw back. They plan too much. They wait too long. They try to do too much. They hesitate. They do not have fun. They talk about it too much. They miss the moment. The possibility is gone. They talk themselves out of the future God has both promised and given to them.

Dying congregations do not discover and live out even one or two of the seven paradigm shifts. They pretend the future has not come. They reject the gifts God seeks to give to them. They do not think about the possibility of considering that they could live out even some of the paradigm shifts. They deny. They resist. They dig in. They become determined not to change, advance, and grow. They walk away from the future God has both promised and given to them. They turn their backs on God.

Weak, declining, and dying congregations do this:

- They think, plan, behave, act, and live as an institution, not a movement.

- They share the motivations of challenge, reasonability, and commitment more than compassion, community, and hope. The first three are their majors; the second three are their minors.

- They ignore the discoveries of the universe we are making and discourage people from trying to make sense of living in this universe and on this planet.

- They help people grow with a primary focus on solid marathon runner possibilities, and they deprecate excellent sprinter possibilities.

- They primarily offer mission projects that are indirect, conserving, too much (too little), and top-down, and only secondarily opportunities that are direct, generous, just enough, and grassroots.

- With a quiet controlling, directing spirit, they know what is best for people. They direct people as to what they should do rather than help people to discover their own best creativity and developing objectives for which they have ownership.

- They emphasize an inside-the-church life, a parts view of life, rather than encouraging people to discover and live the whole of life.

Congregations that focus on these traits do not reach and grow the grass roots. When they continue with these patterns of behavior, they become weak and declining, and eventually dying. They contribute little to God's mission. They have a theology of survival. They may be small and weak, middle and dying, or large and declining congregations.

The grassroots people sense that such congregations are not able to help them with their life's journey in this new time. In effect the grass roots say, "This congregation has decided not to grow and benefit from these paradigm shifts. Then how can it help me grow and benefit from these paradigm shifts in my own life?" This is not said in an accusatory tone. More often, it is said in a sad, wistful, wishful spirit: "I wish this congregation could have helped me. They seem like nice people. I wish them well."

Such congregations have not discovered, are not living out the new paradigm shifts in their thinking and planning, feeling and dreaming, behaving and living. They are ill. They are dying. They live with the past that has been rather than the future that has come. They die with the past that has been rather than live with the future that has come.

We honor their choice. Some people do decide to dwell on the past in the present. The past is gone, but they choose to live in the present as though the past still existed. We do not threaten them. We do not ridicule them. We do not chastise them. We share compassion, community, and hope. We share the wisdom and experience of our own pilgrimage, of what we have learned and are learning about this future that has come. We share our experience with humility and generosity, grateful that God gives us the gift of living in this remarkable time.

God gives you the choice. You can live with the future that has come. You can help your congregation do likewise. A helpful way forward is to:

1. Claim the paradigm shifts you have already made.
2. Expand one of them. Build on your strengths. Do better what you do best. Advance one of the paradigm shifts you have already made. To expand it, look for

two creative objectives that help you advance this paradigm shift in your life.

3. Add one new paradigm shift. Select one you are near to, almost already achieving. Look for two to four creative objectives that help you add this paradigm shift in your life.

4. Act on your future. Know God's grace is stirring in your life.

Develop four of the paradigm shifts in your own life—ultimately, over time, not all at once. You will live a rich, full, abundant life. In your enthusiasm to grow, do not allow that old, old friend, a compulsion toward perfectionism, to show up yet another time in your life. Leave that old friend behind. Yes, look to four in the future. For now, expand one; add one. Have fun. You will thrive.

When you find your way to four of the seven paradigm shifts, you discover two things happen. One, you are having so much fun with the four that the other three do not matter. Two, you are having so much fun with the four that a spill-over effect happens. The four with which you are having fun, with spillover impact, are helping the other three come along.

Think of the four you will have fun developing in your life. For you, it is a certain four. For another person, it is yet another four. For someone else, it is yet another four. No two people grow forward in exactly the same way. The same is true for congregations. No two congregations grow forward in exactly the same way. We grow forward in distinctive ways. Discover the four that work for you.

The spirit of this approach is grace. To focus on all seven is law. God shares grace with us. We can share grace with ourselves and with one another. This list of paradigm possibilities helps. I encourage you to focus on the future that has come.

The Future That Has Come	**The Past That Has Been**
We think, plan, behave, act, and live as a movement.	We think, plan, behave, act, and live as an institution.
We share the motivations of compassion, community, and hope.	We share the motivations of challenge, reasonability, commitment.
We encourage people to make sense of life in this universe and on this planet.	We ignore the discoveries of the universe we are making.
We help people grow with a balance of excellent sprinter and solid marathon runner possibilities, and we value all of them.	We help people grow with a primary focus on solid marathon runner possibilities. We deprecate excellent sprinter ones.
We encourage people to participate in mission that is direct, generous, just enough, and grassroots.	We primarily offer mission projects that are indirect, conserving, too much, (not enough), and top-down.
We help people to discover their best creativity and objectives for which they have ownership.	We know what is best for people. In a quiet, controlling, directing manner, we direct people as to what they should do.
We encourage people to discover and live the whole of life.	We have a focus on the parts and emphasize an inside-the-church life.

Underline the paradigm shifts you have already made in your life.

Double underline one of those that you have underlined, which you would have fun expanding, growing forward.

Circle one new paradigm shift (not underlined) you would have fun growing as a new strength.

Act on your future.

Look first to see what you are doing well. People make this mistake when they look at the list of paradigm possibilities. They look to see what they are "doing wrong." They look at the paradigm shifts they are not doing well. They head to their weakest weaknesses. They try to fix them. They try to be sure they have all seven paradigm shifts in place. You do not need all seven. Expand one. Add one. Head toward four.

Live as a movement. Share compassion, community, and hope. Encourage people to make sense of living in this universe and the discoveries we are making of it. Help people grow a balance of excellent sprinter and solid marathon runner behavior patterns. Encourage people to participate in mission projects that are direct, generous, just enough, and grassroots. Help people discover their best creativity and objectives. Encourage yourself and others to live the whole of life. Do four of these. You will grow yourself. You will reach and grow the grass roots.

∞

Julie and I were on a trip together. We were in the capital city of a restful, enchanting country. The people are gracious. The hillsides are green. Open spaces abound. We were having great fun. Both of us enjoy peaceful, adventurous exploring. We had a hired car. We headed out to see the remote regions of the country. We got the best map we could find. We decided to head north, to the outer reaches of the country, to see where the land met the ocean.

I noticed on the map that the modest paved road in the city quickly gave way, just beyond the city, to a little dirt road. I traced the road. The dirt road continued for a while, getting narrower; then, on the map, the word "unknown" was written. Several times. The map maker wanted people to know they would now be in the unknown.

The dirt road on which we planned to travel seemed to end at what looked like a tree. On the map, by the drawing of the tree, there were two words: "Black Stump." I asked the person who sold us the map what that meant. She said, "The black stump is our way of saying that past this point is beyond the end of forever." I noted to her that, on the map, the distance from the black stump on north to the edge of the ocean looked to be a considerable number of miles. I asked, "Is there a road on to the ocean?" With a twinkle in her eyes, she said, "You be surprised. Enjoy your trip."

Julie and I headed out. Time and miles passed. We passed through a wonderful countryside with rolling hills and ancient trees. We came to the black stump. It was off to the side of the road, a huge old tree stump, black, withered, worn, still strong. The dirt road on which we had been traveling continued, much to our delight and surprise. It was very narrow and quite bumpy.

We said, "Well, it's not on the map, but here it is. Let's give it a go."

We found ourselves traveling in some of the most beautiful parts of that country. The trees seemed taller and greener. The grass was richer and thicker. We saw more birds and wildlife, but no people. No one seemed to live there. After a long time, the road made a turn to the left, and as we came around the bend, we saw an ancient, stately lighthouse, with a small, whitewashed, now empty cottage beside it.

We pulled our hired car to a stop and got out. A peaceful quiet surrounded us. A bird now and then lifted its voice in song. We walked around the lighthouse and stood at the edge of the shore. There, we saw the most amazing sight. Two separate seas came together and joined as one just off that coast. One had a rich, coral color, the other a brighter, deeper blue. The sun shone brightly, dancing across the gently rolling waves. It was as if we had discovered a completely new world.

God's steadfast love endures forever . . . even beyond the end of forever. God gives us this New World. The grace of God surrounds us. The compassion of Christ sustains us. The hope of the Holy Spirit leads us. We live whole, healthy lives. God invites us to new possibilities to reach and grow the grass roots. God blesses us with the future that has come.

May the grace of God, the compassion of Christ, and the hope of the Holy Spirit be with you and yours, now and beyond the end of forever. God bless you.

The Author

Kennon L. Callahan—researcher, professor, and pastor—is today's most sought-after church consultant and speaker. He has worked with thousands of congregations around the world and has helped tens of thousands of church leaders and pastors. His dynamic seminars are filled with wisdom and practical possibilities. Author of many books, he is best known for his groundbreaking *Twelve Keys to an Effective Church,* which has formed the basis for the widely acclaimed Mission Growth Movement, which is helping congregations across the world.

Callahan has earned B.A., M.Div., S.T.M., and Ph.D. degrees; his doctorate is in systematic theology. He has served as a pastor of rural and urban congregations in Ohio, Texas, and Georgia and taught for many years at Emory University.

He and his wife, Julia, have two children, Ken and Mike, and three grandchildren, Blake, Mason, and Brice. They enjoy the outdoors, hiking, horseback riding, camping, hammered dulcimer music, sailing, and quilting. They live in Dallas.

Index